THE LIFE AND TIMES OF
ANNIE WILLIAMS

Last of a Fenland Dynasty

Mike Heath

THE LIFE AND TIMES OF ANNIE WILLIAMS

Copyright ©2021

Mike Heath has asserted his right under the Copyright Designs and Patents Act 1988 to be identified as the author of this work.

This book is dedicated to Sandra, my wife, who has been my rock and supported me at every stage. Σε αγαπώ

CONTENTS

Preface
Acknowledgments
Introduction

1. Annie and the Decoy 1
- Life at the Decoy

2. Early Memories .. 9
- A Simple Life
- Peterborough
- Ice Skating
- Daily Chores

3. Annie Starts School 21
- Trains and Trams
- Dame School
- An Awful Fatality
- Victoria's Diamond Jubilee
- Sunday, Day of Worship
- Seaside Visit
- Boer War
- Death of Queen Victoria
- Annie's First Bicycle
- Health Matters
- Kettering High School
- Back Home
- Peterborough Agricultural Show
- Edward VII and Alexandra
- George V and Mary
- First Aeroplane to Land at Peterborough
- Special Celebrations
- Crowland floods

4. The War Years 53
- Peakirk and the War
- Wartime Nurse
- Home
- Enter Billy Williams

5. Back home 67
- Rook Shooting
- The Postwar Era
- Annie and Billy get married
- European ventures
- Fashion
- Votes for Women
- Social Life
- Cinema and Entertainment
- The General Strike
- The Depression
- Abdication, 1936

6. Enter Peter Scott 104 91
- Annie Becomes an Artist
- Beer and Pubs

7. Into the Second World War 101
- Observer Corps
- Rationing
- Wartime Radio
- Wartime Entertainment
- Blackout Mishap
- Aftermath of the War

8. The Estate Sold Off 117
- Arthur Hill
- Crowland
- 1947 Floods
- Return of Winston Churchill
- An Unwelcome Move
- A Treasure Trove

9. The End of a Dynasty 135
- Rest in Peace

Postscript 139
Appendix A   Borough Fen Decoy Farm House 141
Appendix B   Closure 143
Appendix C   Local Area Map 145
Appendix D   Williams Family Tree 146
Appendix E   The Peakirk Neighbourhood 147
             Plan 2016 – 2030
Appendix F   Money Conversion 151

Photos and Acknowledgements 152
Bibliography 155
Index 156

PREFACE

I am a retired history teacher and have undertaken various local history projects over the years. For example, I've studied the growth and development of Peterborough from a sleepy little city into an important industrial site as a direct result of the railways arriving and revitalizing the place. My interest in local history led me to being invited to write the life story of Annie Williams, which, rather belatedly, I have done.

My brother Paul introduced me to Annie. He was living in a cottage in Crowland that had belonged to Will, Annie's husband, and it passed to her on Will's death. Paul used to travel to Peakirk to pay Annie his £3 a week rent and he soon became friendly with her. The following, from Paul, speaks volumes about her character:

"I once expressed a concern about her leaving the key in her door. She sent me upstairs to search in a trunk for a small pistol. She asked if I could obtain ammunition for her so she could shoot any intruders. Fortunately, it was so old, ammunition of that calibre was no longer available. She opted to keep it by her side and just threaten people instead."

Between 1975 and 1976, I conducted over a dozen two-hour interviews with Annie Williams and, despite many questions posed to her, she never once repeated herself. I had the opportunity to follow up on several historical events that she witnessed or took part in, and the facts were

Will Williams' cottage

borne out exactly as she had recalled. I found this to be a remarkable feat for someone aged 85. I tape-recorded all of the interviews to aid my note taking and would have kept them, as it was fascinating to hear history being recounted first hand.

Annie had a cheerful little budgerigar whose constant chirping could be heard throughout. The human ear can close out such sounds, but my old tape recorder wasn't quite sophisticated enough to cancel out the incessant chirruping, so transcribing the tapes occasionally became an unpleasant experience.

When she was expecting me for an interview session, Annie would leave the door of her house unlocked, so that I could let myself in. By that time she experienced difficulty in walking, though her mind was as sharp as ever and her hearing unimpaired. She would call out from her sitting room, "Come on in, Michael. It's good to see you again". Thankfully, I was never threatened with a pistol.

The renowned ornithologist Sir Peter Scott had lived with Annie and Billy in their house at Borough Fen in 1932 and had many dealings with the family over the years following. He was a renowned artist and had a wonderful pencil sketch of Annie which I was hoping to use as a cover for the book if it ever got published. He answered a number of questions for me about Annie and the Decoy, and had agreed to write the foreword although, sadly, Sir Peter passed away in 1989, long before I was ready to publish the book.

ACKNOWLEDGEMENTS

Special thanks to my wife Sandra, who accompanied me to all the interviews and has helped with constructive suggestions; my son Chris, for the photography and constant encouragement; to Sheila Lever (churchwarden) at St Pega's, Peakirk for sterling research work often beyond the call of duty; Sandra Pledger, who used to work with Annie and was a very useful source provider and proof reader; Ann Fletcher, former resident of the Decoy Farm house, who provided much essential information and some valuable photographs; Colin Paterson; for permission to use two excellent photographs; Peterborough Oldies Facebook page; Lynda Stimson; the late Sir Peter Scott for his invaluable help at the time; Dafila Scott (Peter's daughter), who was also particularly helpful; Angela Hankins, Clerk to Peakirk Parish Council; John Arbon, whose great uncle was a decoy man under Billy Williams; Peterborough Images Archive for the permission they gave for the use of many of the photos; Ellie Wise at the Wildfowl and Wetlands Trust, Slimbridge; and Kathryn Jones and Robert Waddington at the Lincolnshire Archives. Very special thanks, too, for the very many sensible suggestions and advice from Stephanie Rouse. Greg Morton from WGM Atlantic also gave up time and provided me with professional advice.

Last, but certainly not least, is my brother Paul, who introduced me to Annie and suggested that I write her life story.

INTRODUCTION

I was amazed at the clarity with which Annie recounted events from her life even from eighty years past. She was a very forthright woman, not necessarily openly championing women's rights but certainly eager to do what she wanted to do. I was struck when she claimed, "I was quite equal to any man", and I believed her.

She was a very determined young woman and continued this way all through her lifetime. She never really lived the stereotypical life of a genteel countrywoman. She was well educated and took an interest in many things you would not expect from a person in her position.

Her life out in the middle of nowhere in Fenland was never dull, and in her frequent visits to Peterborough or London she experienced a wide variety of things. She met or encountered many people who have been very important in the history of this country. Her long-lasting relationship with Peter Scott, the renowned naturalist and painter, was probably the key one. "I used to darn his socks when he was at the Decoy" perhaps sums up the strength of their friendship best.

As the world changed from Victorian England through a brutal First World War and then another against the tyranny of Nazism into a more liberal society where she had "no time for long-haired men", she continued to enjoy life and a happy and enduring relationship with her husband Will. Life on the farm and the Decoy had always been hard, but she was energetic in pursuit of whatever needed to be done. Her place as the very last in a three-hundred-year dynasty of decoy folk will last forever.

She was briefly a nurse during the First World War and helped out in the floods that beset the fenland, particularly the one in Crowland in 1947. She was an active witness to a number of epoch-making events. Her discovery of the joy of painting under the early tutelage of Peter Scott, her visits to the theatre, her love of flowers and her work at the Wildfowl Trust in Peakirk are all related here.

When Annie was born, women were outsiders to the formal structures of political life. They did not have the vote. They could not serve on juries nor hold any elective office. They were not part of the growing Trade Union movement. They were, in reality, second-class citizens. The 1911 Census shows that almost 30% of all employed women were engaged in domestic service and many more in the 'sweated industries' of factory life. Married women had the stereotypical role of the stay-at-home mother bringing up the children while the husband was the breadwinner for the family.

Annie lived a privileged life, and while not a pioneer for women's rights, she lived her life as she wanted, as we shall see.

I have written her story as she told it to me, with lots of her words verbatim and within speech marks. I have been able to verify virtually everything that she told me by meticulous research, but I am prepared to accept that some of her recollections may not have been 100% accurate. She did hold very forthright views on many things, like

England's place in the world, the monarchy, Winston Churchill, the Conservative Party and the way the world today has become much too reliant on money.

I was very honoured to have met her and to have had the opportunity to tell her story. God bless her. God bless Annie Williams.

Chapter 1

ANNIE AND THE DECOY

―――

Annie Williams was the last in a long line of the Williams family dating back to the reign of King Charles II. They lived at the Decoy from 1670, when it was constructed, until Annie's time three centuries later.

I think it would be prudent to give a detailed explanation of what a decoy actually is, and how it works. I propose to take the liberty of quoting 'in extensor' a very relevant and informative section from Sir Peter Scott in the famous naturalist's book *The Eye of the Wind*. He witnessed the process first-hand when living at the decoy in 1932. Much later, when the decoy's economy permitted them to kill no more birds, Sir Peter and Will 'Billy' Williams initiated a programme to ring and release the catch. This was much more agreeable and humane, without a doubt.

The following is Sir Peter Scott's description of the decoy.

The decoy wood lay 200 yards from the farmhouse – 18 acres of trees, among them tall poplars, elms and oaks standing out in the vast bare expanse of fenland fields. Inside the wood was a small secret pond of 2½ acres, of a regular but complex shape. It had eight very small bays, from which led eight curved tapering ditches each about 60 yards long and five yards wide at the mouth. The ditches were sparred by hoops made of ash or willow saplings, over which tarred string netting was stretched to make a tapering tunnel, curving to the right as it went farther from the open water of the pond.

Along the outside of the curve were ranged a row of screens made of reeds three or four yards long and six feet high, set up in an overlapping pattern like a venetian blind, which could be seen through from one direction but not the other. These eight devices, radiating from the central pool were called the 'pipes' and Borough Fen was, therefore, an eight-pipe decoy (as illustrated opposite).

To operate a decoy, it is necessary to entice some of the ducks which have collected on the pond (often in thousands) to come into a pipe, and this may be achieved in three ways. First the banks of the pond can be made vertical except in the pipes, so that the ducks which want to go ashore and preen and sleep can do so only on the 'landings' in the pipe or at its mouth; this is called 'banking' Alternatively, the birds may be encouraged to come to the pipes with food spread on the 'landings' But the most surprising and

BOROUGH FEN DECOY

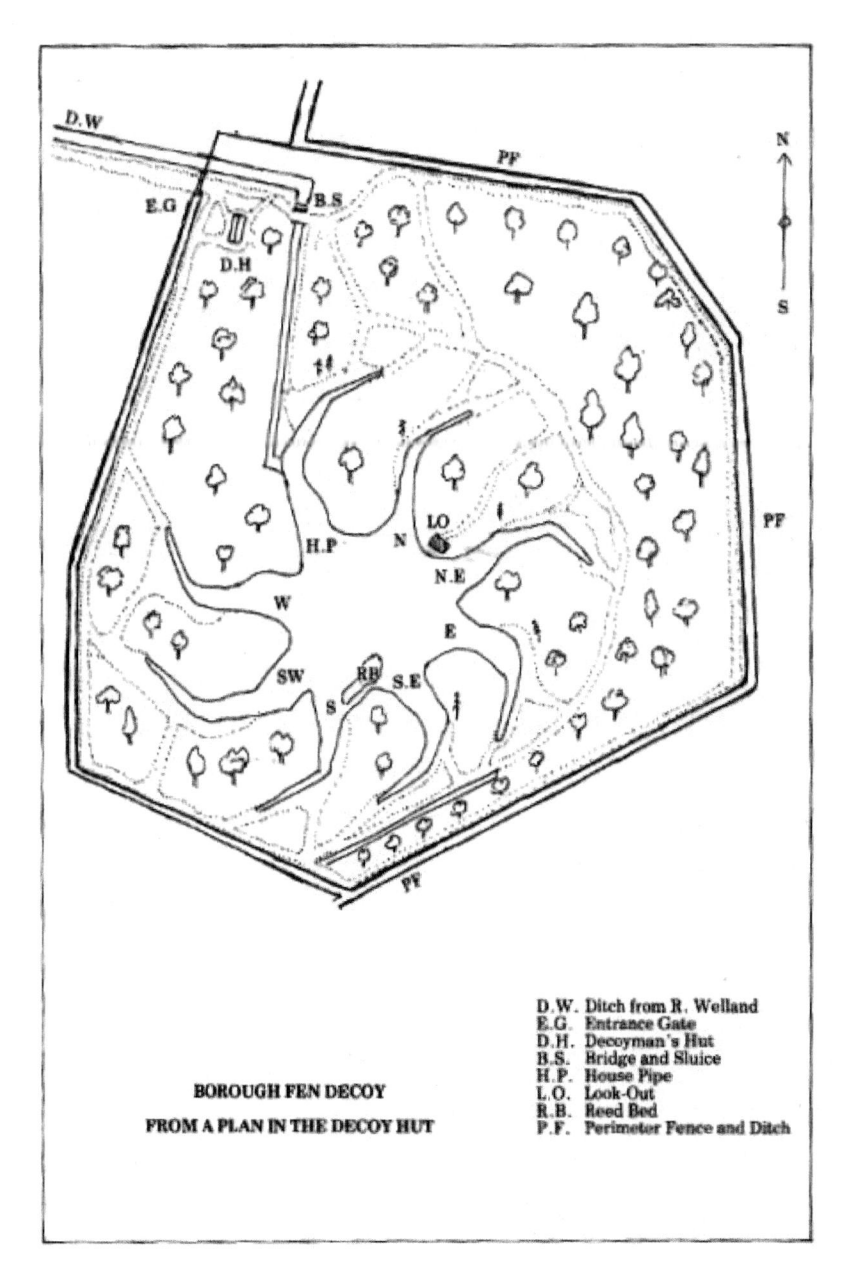

FROM A PLAN IN THE DECOY HUT

D.W. Ditch from R. Welland
E.G. Entrance Gate
D.H. Decoyman's Hut
B.S. Bridge and Sluice
H.P. House Pipe
L.O. Look-Out
R.B. Reed Bed
P.F. Perimeter Fence and Ditch

interesting method is the use of a trained dog. In this the decoy man exploits the curious behaviour pattern of ducks in the presence of a predator. If, for example, a fox appears before them when they are sitting on the water, they appear to feel safe enough to swim up within a few feet and mob it. The attraction seems to be all the greater if the predatory animal is retreating.

The application of this principle in Holland in the 16th Century is still the operating basis for most of the duck decoys which remain in existence. The dog is trained to run around the overlapping screens, appearing and retreating along the screen, disappearing again progressively farther and farther up the pipe as the ducks follow it. At Borough Fen, as in many other decoys, the dog jumps over a two-foot high screen called a 'dog leap' and appears again with startling suddenness, which seems to be even more stimulating. The 'dog leaps' occupy the space between the ends of the high screens making, in plan view, a zig-zag pattern.

When as many ducks as possible have been lured under the archway of netting, the decoy man appears suddenly at the mouth of the pipe. Because of the overlap of the screens he is still invisible to the ducks out on the pool, but is in full view of those in the pipe. They dare not fly back towards him for he appears to have cut off their retreat to the open pond. Instead they fly away from him up the pipe, thinking perhaps to escape round the bend, but there they find the pipe growing ever narrower. The decoy man is following close behind them as they run up the final slope from the narrow channel, into the detachable tubular net at the pipe's end. From this tunnel net, they are removed, and in the days when I first went to the Borough Fen decoy they were speedily killed and sent to market in London. Nowadays Borough Fen decoy and some others (including our four- pipe decoy at Slimbridge – built in 1845) are used *exclusively for ringing and measuring ducks, which are then released.*

Life at the Decoy

One interesting fact about the decoy and how it worked involved the technique of training tame ducks to respond to the decoy man's whistle, which would induce others to follow. There was also the practice of using carved wooden decoy ducks, and later inflatable rubber and plastic ones.

Until the railway age from the late 1840s, the birds that were sent to London were carried by horse to Norman Cross on the Great North Road (16 miles away), and thence by stagecoach. Birds caught in the afternoon could arrive at London's Leadenhall Market by the next morning. They were usually packed in hampers made from osiers grown in Peakirk (the site of Annie's house). The osier was a willow basket. These birds were in much better condition than those which had been shot, having had their necks expertly dislocated. Cooks in London much preferred the decoy birds, as they looked neater and kept fresh longer than those which had been shot. This was a major advantage in those days before refrigeration.

I mentioned earlier that the connection between the Williams family and the Borough Fen Decoy dates back to the time of the 'Merry Monarch', Charles II. They had lived at the decoy from 1670, when it was built for the Earl of Lincoln.

Before I recount Annie's very interesting life story it would be useful to put her story into context by briefly devoting some space to her illustrious ancestors over the preceding three hundred years.

An excellent article on the decoy appeared in the *Peterborough Advertiser* (7th December, 1928). One of the main points put forward was that to visitors, the decoy man was less interesting than what he decoyed. H.R.P., the author of the article, pleaded a strong case for the "amazing romance of people engaged in the decoy system". To him the literary-cum-scientific visitors were *far more concerned with the bare fact that 20 dozen duck was an average take than with the romantic idea of the decoy being made by a Williams in 1670 and the family living there ever since, being born, growing up to become decoy men, marrying the daughters of neighbouring farmers and finally being buried in Peakirk Churchyard.*"

A table of the principal dates is included in the article, which I reproduce below, having added a number of the later dates myself.

1670	Decoy constructed by a Williams for the Earl of Lincoln
1692	Andrew Williams, "who served the Lloyds of Aston, Shropshire" 60 years as a decoy man, was born. He died in 1776.
1710	John Williams (described in his will as a 'gent' of High Borough Fen) was born.
1776	John was taking an average of 10 dozen 'winter fowle' every four days

1777	John was taking an average of 28 dozen 'summer fowle' every four days.
1784	John Williams II selling ham at Crowland
1786	Death of John Williams I
1788	John Williams II selling wildfowl through London salesmen Samuel and James Boyce
1825	John Williams II buried at Peakirk.
1830	Joseph Williams prosecutes Mr Seaton for disturbing his decoy.
1871	Joseph is succeeded by his nephew, J.B. Williams
1890	Annie Williams born 9th September
1900	J.B. Williams succeeded by Herbert Williams (Annie's father)
1920	Annie married Will ('Billy') Williams, 5 April
1929	Death of Herbert, succeeded by Will Williams, his son in law
1957	Billy Williams dies leaving Annie a widow.
1986	Annie, the last of the Williams line, dies aged 96.

The following epitaph, which was much revered and often quoted by the Williams family, was carved on the tombstone of Andrew Williams, the first decoy man:

"Here lies the decoy man, who lived like an otter Dividing his time twixt the land and the water His hide he oft soaked in the waters of Perry. While Aston old beer his spirits kept merry. Amphibious his life, Death was plagued to say How to dust to reduce such well moistened clay; So death turned decoy man and coyed him to land, Where he fixed his abode till quite dried to the hand, He then found him fitting for crumbling to dust, And here he lies mouldering, as you and I must."

It was into this long running family that Annie was born on Tuesday 9th September 1890. This is her story.

Chapter 2

EARLY MEMORIES

Annie's earliest recollection is of having a photograph taken at the age of three. She had her hair cut for this picture, and it was cut straight like a boy's. She remembered, too, a hat she was very fond of. It was a leghorn with a white ostrich feather round it. "Everyone wore a hat. You wouldn't even think of going out into the garden without putting your hat on." At this time her father, Herbert Williams, was working as an assistant to J.B. Williams. Apart from being the decoy man and Annie's grandfather, he was the Surveyor for the Soke of Peterborough. This latter duty took up so much time that Herbert (Annie's father) was at times in reality the decoy man. Annie and her parents did not actually move to the decoy until 1900 when J.B. died. Their home was in Peakirk.

This house was a small bay-windowed building with a room either side of the kitchen and five very small bedrooms – two over each side room and one over the kitchen. The furniture was solidly Victorian. The bedrooms had iron bedsteads and feather mattresses, which were good for sleeping and reputedly bad for one's back.

Annie and her parents spent a lot of time at the decoy farm. Her grandfather was a heavily built, imposing man, and very stern, with a long black beard. He took his duties as a typical Victorian head of the household tremendously seriously. Annie remembers that she had to get down on her knees on the hard floor when J.B. led the family prayers which were a daily occurrence. Sometimes he would read a whole chapter from the Bible as well. Everyone had to attend. He would issue the orders for the day immediately after the lengthy prayer session. It is not surprising to learn that Annie did not like her grandfather. I would imagine that there was a grand sense of relief when he finally died in 1899 aged 79.

Having said that, Annie fondly recalled early Christmases. One year on Christmas Eve she was lying in bed when she was woken by the sound of carol singers outside her window and a rendition of 'Once in Royal David's City' – one of her favourite carols. Christmas was very much a family affair then. They had their goose or turkey in the afternoon followed by a dessert composed of fruits – "oranges, apples, prunes in a bottle, nuts and raisins". Presents were always hung in a black stocking with an orange in the toe, sugar mice, lots of little toys in netting, which were made of wood and of metal, a whip and top: "We liked to draw pretty patterns on the top so that when it spun around it was like a kaleidoscope." Rodgers was a good toy shop – opposite the Post Office in Cumbergate, in Peterborough. "I remember a popular toy was a moveable monkey on a stick. Then there were hoops, tops, marbles and shuttlecocks. There was a time or season in the year for each game. We never celebrated November 5th but Christmas was always a big event."

One Christmas, after her granddad had died, her cousin came come over and slept in the same bedroom with her. The bedroom was over the kitchen and it was in here that the cousin invited the carol singers on one occasion. "She gave them beer and mince pies and we all got very merry." There was dancing and singing. The cousin was charged the next morning with cleaning the mess up from the kitchen floor.

Annie had no one to play with normally. She had dolls but, to her, the main attraction at the Decoy was the wildlife and exploring. She did sometimes play with a boy from a neighbouring farm. He was about the same age and they became friends when the skating season began.

A Simple Life

Life at the Decoy was simple. "Meat was cheap. It had to be, hadn't it?" Almost everyone in the neighbourhood had a pig a year. This was for home-cured ham. As there were no refrigerators, the food was preserved. The dairy was on the north side and always cold. The meat was salted and put into long troughs (about six foot) and salted. Salt and saltpeter were used in a method dating back to the Ancient Greeks. Brown sugar was then rubbed into it to give it a better flavour. It was kept in the dairy for a month and then taken out to be placed in the scullery. There were beams in the roof which were ideal for storing the pork. There was a great open hearth in the scullery and faggots and wood was burnt to dry the meat. It was then taken and stored somewhere cooler and stored in bags. This was during the time when there were no gas lights at the Decoy. It was paraffin lamps and candles only.

The people employed at the Decoy by the Williams family lived in tied cottages. Rent was often minimal and considered part of the employee's remuneration or a 'perk' of the job. There was no electricity, and the lighting came from oil lamps and candles. There would usually be one oil lamp in the middle of the table, so the light was never really strong. For those who could read, the task was made difficult. It was never easy to see to do much. Rainwater was collected in large wooden barrels. A big ladle was used to get some water to drink. There often lots of little squirming insects which you had to miss when scooping the water.

"There was one cottage on Toll Bar, another near The Decoy Pub - then called The Red Cow. There were others there, too." The families would usually be in work. There was not much money about then. The jobs would include yard work and looking after the cows and horses. Of course, at harvest time it was all hands to the pump. Even Annie used to help her mother tie the wheat and corn into sheaves. "We used to call them stooks." She did this for three years. After the wheat was threshed and put into big sacks, it was taken to Maxey Mill to be ground into flour. They were given one sack which would last them all winter.

Annie's father used to collect water from a borehole on a neighbouring farm (Whitsed's) with two buckets on a yoke. This was done every night because the water was used for drinking. The land in the area was gravelly and good for getting water. Wells could be 20 feet deep. There were also pumps in Peakirk village. Some water was obtained from dykes. "You used a pump and there was also a filter to get rid of the sticklebacks etc." Rainwater, which was "nice and soft", was also collected, as at the tied cottages, and they had big filters on to prevent the insects getting in. Soda was added, which was good for washing and cooking vegetables. "It kept the cabbages green". Bathing was in a tin bath and the water was usually shared. Going last was never too good. The bath was placed in front of the fireplace. Some of the local farm children used to bathe in the River Welland near Peakirk – no thoughts of swimming pools in those days for these children. It must have been more fun than waiting your turn in the tin bath, especially if you were last!

Coal was also burnt. The railway revolution of the 1840s and '50s saw Peterborough develop greatly and much coal was stored, usually down from Doncaster on the Great Northern Line. It would be brought to Peakirk by horse and cart at £5 for 10 tons. "This would generally get the household through till spring. There was never a shortage of wood, which the Decoy itself could provide. It was this wood and coal that kept the Decoy properly heated during the winter months.

"There was a great range for cooking. Nothing like it." It took a hundredweight of coal to cook a big family dinner.

It also provided hot water, as the boiler was on the go all of the time.

"We had our main meal at midday. Pudding was eaten first because we didn't eat so much meat in those days. We would have roly poly puddings and other boiled puddings. We also had lots of soups made with the bones of animals to make a good stock. We didn't make bread but got it twice a week when the baker with his horse and cart came from Newborough. The only drawback to this was that if there was bad weather then he didn't come. Milk we got from our own cows. I used to help out in the dairy. I did used to make the butter and then sell some for a shilling a pound, which was a good price."

There were hard times in the winter. Some families had only casual labourers and the aforementioned bad weather would mean no work. There was a 'Poor Rate' and people went 'on the parish'. Money came out of the rates. This was felt most by agriculture workers. The growth of industry in Peterborough, for example Peter Brotherhoods, meant that some people who left the countryside were able to move into a more comfortable world. "Some people even bought grand pianos, even if they could not play, just for the sake of appearances."

Peterborough

Fashion before the First World War was very much on the Victorian model. Children, including Annie, wore white starched pinafores. She remembers the short-lived fashion of hobble skirts, which were tight at the bottom and designed to prevent the wearer taking anything but small steps. "It was done to make you walk like a lady." Hats were always fashionable and Annie recalled buying a huge straw hat, in a sale, one summer. "I cycled home. It was quite windy and by the time I reached home the hat was bent all over the place. My friends, who were sitting on the lawn, roared with laughter when they saw me."

Peterborough was the place to go for clothing. Barretts was a very popular shop, as was Thompson's. The most exclusive fashion shop was called Claribus, on Market Square." It was quite expensive. It had great mannequin dummies in the windows." After you had paid for your goods, the sales assistant would place the money and any paperwork in a cylindrical metal carrier, which could be closed by twisting the ends. Next the carrier was inserted into a metal box known as a 'cash station'. It then whizzed round the shop in tubes by what was called a pneumatic tube system, which worked like a vacuum cleaner, with great suction. This was an Edwardian device. "We didn't need much furniture then but the main shop for this was Williamsons. There were no supermarkets in those days, just big general stores. Dandy was the big, high-class butcher's shop. There were other good shops, too, like Sangsters, Liptons and Maypoles."

There was also a shop called Beavers near the Eastern Carpet Store. "It was great for buns. The man that ran it used to wear a Sherlock Holmes-style hat." A view of Narrow Street in Peterborough, which later became the much wider Bridge Street.

This was the site of the Penny Bazaar which Annie used

A view of Narrow Street in Peterborough, which later became the much wider Bridge Street.

to frequent. You can also see the Angel Hotel, where she attended tea dances later on.

Wednesdays and Saturdays saw the Peterborough Market, held in the very centre of the city opposite the Cathedral." There were fish stalls all the way down towards the Corn Exchange. Many of the stall holders came from Kings Lynn. There was a tap there with running water so that the eels could be skinned. I remember, too, the old shrimp man who had a big basket on his arm." The rest of the market had stalls for the traditional fruit and vegetables. It was a really busy place with people regularly coming in from many miles away.

"On Saturdays what used to make a visit to the market really worthwhile was going to Turners Fish and Chip shop on Market Square. You made your order downstairs and

A postcard of the old market

went up the stairs to enjoy your meal. It cost thruppence (3d) for a piece of fish and chips. I needed this big meal because I often made my own way back home. My father would have brought me in via pony and trap but because he would spend the whole day in town, I went home either walking or the train to Peakirk."

A postcard of the old market

Annie's father, Herbert, has been dubbed the greatest decoy man of the many generations of Williams. Like his father he was efficient, but without the pomposity of J.B. The decoy became his life. He laid out gardens at the farmhouse and added new paths in the decoy, which he bordered with climbing roses and a variety of flowering shrubs. He maintained the pipes and screens of the decoy to a really high degree and kept the paths levelled and mown. He would clear away twigs from the pathways in case the sound of a twig breaking underfoot alarmed the ducks.

Annie told how he would always take a piece of burning peat with him. The theory behind this was that it would drown the smell of human beings. Peat was quite commonly used in the cottages on the area and the ducks, therefore, would sense no alarm – or at least that was the theory. She also recalled how one day when the wind was blowing from the farm to the pond, he came into the house in a rage and went straight to the kitchen at the smell of burning. He wasn't worried that it might be his dinner burning but rather that it might alarm the ducks.

Ice Skating

Herbert's many accomplishments included prowess at ice skating and in Annie's words "before he became too stout", he had been a champion in that traditional fenland winter sport. The Crowland and Cowbit Washes would freeze over and skaters from all over Britain would take part in the Fenland Championships. In winning the One Mile event he beat the legendary 'Turkey' Smart. The prizes for which the skaters competed were a cocked hat, a pig or a purse containing from £1 to £20, which was a small fortune in those days. The races in each event were heats where two skaters were matched with each other after being drawn by ballot. The races were run until just two skaters were left to contend for the prize. Because there was little, if any, work at this time, some of the farm workers used to charge people 2d a time to put their skates on for them. They were screwed to your shoe and a screw placed in the hole in the heel of the shoe. They were then strapped on tightly.

There were no big wages at that time. "A farm labourer would earn fifteen shillings a week, an under-horse keeper thirteen shillings and a boy (just out of school) would get eight shillings. It was just enough for them to live on."

'Turkey' Smart, perhaps the finest racer of his day, was often backed for money to break the two-minute barrier for the mile. Despite numerous attempts, the closest he ever came to success was just two seconds over the two-minute limit. For Herbert to beat this highly regarded skater was certainly an achievement to be proud of. Annie took great delight in recounting this story.

Daily Chores

Annie's mother, Elizabeth Ann, was a well-mannered woman of few words. She ran her household with quiet precision but, while she tolerated no deviation from routine, she seldom raised more than an eyebrow in reprimand. That eyebrow carried more weight than any scolding.

Life in the farmhouse would begin at 7 am with the skimming of the milk. Each day was assigned to a particular household chore. Monday the washing, Tuesday the ironing and the churning for butter, Wednesday the bedrooms and parlour, Thursday the kitchen and so on. "We used to fetch a woman from Peakirk to do the washing once a month and she was paid a shilling a day."

Washing was done in a copper. Everything was washed and rubbed and put in the copper to boil. A starch solution was added and it was stirred with a long wooden stick before being hung out to dry. The following day it would be ironed. The flat iron was heated on top of the oven or in front of an open roaring fire. Elizabeth Williams was, of course, acting in the same way as did countless other housewives throughout the land – an ordinary housewife.

Chapter 3

ANNIE STARTS SCHOOL

⎯⎯⎯⎯⎯⎯

Annie first went to school at the age of five. Every morning she walked the two miles from the Decoy to Glinton to attend the village primary school, and every evening she made the return journey. There were bicycles in those days, but certainly no cars or school buses. Children thought nothing of walking long distances; it was expected and accepted practice. Depending on the time of year the journey both ways could be in darkness, as she set off before 8 am. There was no daylight saving then.

There were no toilets at the school, just 'privies'. If it rained while you were going to school, in the winter especially you could remain wet. Feet in particular remained wet all day. The heating was from old combustion stoves. "If you were lucky and got on well with the teacher, you could sit near to it."

This independence of youth was further illustrated two

years later when Annie became a regular traveller to Peterborough on her own at the tender age of seven. She would board a train at Peakirk Station, after paying the fare of tuppence ha'penny, and journey alone to Peterborough North Station. No one came to meet her. She would proceed on foot to Cromwell Road, where she used to lodge with her mother's cousin. She attended a small school there during the week, travelling back on a Friday. Attendance at this school lasted only a short time, for Annie soon found herself at a dame school, a type of girls' school of the time run by elderly women, in Lincoln Road East.

The travel arrangements were the same again. She would catch the 8.45 am train into Peterborough. She returned for weekends on the 4.45 pm train to Peakirk and her father met her and took this intrepid young commuter home in a pony and trap. She remembered that most of the weekend was spent in a gastronomic orgy: "I ate until I made myself ill". Needless to say, the food at Lincoln Road East was quite scarce – not enough for a growing healthy country girl.

Annie went to stay with one of her cousins in Peterborough while she was at school in the city. The address was Star Road, right in the midst of the slum area Boongate (or Bun Git as the locals called it) She walked from the Market Place through the cloisters of the Cathedral and one day she witnessed a man "beating a woman up. There was blood everywhere. I was frightened to death and dare not look at the man. In those days there was little police presence so I hurried past to get to my cousin's house".

Trains and Trams

Peakirk Railway Station opened as Peakirk & Crowland in 1848 and was renamed simply Peakirk in 1871. It survived through to 1961, when it closed, despite the line continuing to see service.

Trams were first introduced to Peterborough in 1903, when Annie was still a schoolgirl. She said that her father never entertained the concept and did his best to subvert the system. There were three routes. The main one ran from Walton into Westgate in the city centre. "My father always took his horse and trap when he went into Peterborough and deliberately travelled over the tram lines along Lincoln Road. He refused to move off, keeping the tram waiting behind him. He was adamant that he was not going to move, even when the tram driver rang his bell. He took no notice. Eventually my father and the driver became good friends. It was taken in good fun. My father bought him a drink or two. He certainly was a bit of a character.

"He used to go into the city on a Saturday to buy his tobacco. He would use the Bull Inn, in Westgate, as a base. He never carried any parcels or packages. He would buy cheese from Sangster's after trying all the different sorts and then asked for biscuits to go with them. He would have them all sent to the Bull, where he would make his final choice. This was his way of having a good feed for nothing. Very canny, my dad".

In those days, on a Saturday in Peterborough, you would meet up with other farmers and most shops had their regular customers. "Everybody knew everybody in those days." The trams stopped in 1931. Cars were becoming more common and a bus service had been running since the end of the First World War anyway. It cost 6d from the Red Cow at Milking Nook, near Newborough, in a single decker into Peterborough.

Dame School

The dame school was typical of others in the area at that time. It was run by an elderly spinster schoolteacher called Miss Pope in Lincoln Road East, Peterborough. Annie described her as having her hair strictly swept up and fastened in a bun. She had narrow slanted eyes. This look helped to build the "no nonsense" approach which was typical of the late Victorian era. Annie called her "a rum old girl" and recalled that she certainly liked to drink. She thought the other girls didn't notice but "I recognised that she was drunk on a number of occasions".

There were only a handful of girls at the school. There

was no official uniform as such but "we all wore a starched white pinafore". The building was a private, bay-windowed house and lessons took place in the upstairs front bedroom. Most of the time was taken up with the three 'Rs' (reading, writing and 'rithmetic). There was very little reference to other subjects with the exception of music. Miss Pope did have a piano. Annie wryly confessed that she did not excel at music. The pupils had their own books to write in – one for dictation, one for spelling and so on.

Discipline was very good, which is perhaps not too surprising from young Victorian ladies. There was little thought of disobeying parents and teachers. Annie was, in her own words, "a shy little thing" anyway. She was certainly a strong advertisement for the then popular saying that "little children should be seen but not heard". There was no corporal punishment at Lincoln Road East, though Annie remembers that previously at Glinton, the teacher did use the cane, though not on her, I hasten to add.

Early in Queen Victoria's reign, over one sixth of all schools in England were dame schools, but by 1897 they were dying out and were already an anachronism. Miss Pope's type of private school was on its way out. Some resembled the cosy image of well-scrubbed infants as portrayed in Charles Kingsley's "Water Babies", while many others were run in the cellars of the large cities to accommodate children whose parents were at work. The 1870 Forster's Act changed the face of schooling by initiating a full-scale public system of education, which was certainly necessary.

Annie Witnesses an Awful Fatality

On 5th August 1895, at the age of five, Annie was witness to what the *Peterborough Advertiser* called an "awful fatality to a lady parachutist at Peterborough". She had been staying with relatives at Orton on the outskirts of Peterborough. She was travelling by pony and trap back through Peterborough to the Decoy when it happened. she witnessed the death of It was a Bank Holiday Monday and a crowd of about 10,000 people had gathered at the fete in Fletton to witness what was called the "Race for Life", in which Mademoiselle Adelaide Bassett. would ascend in a balloon filled with gas, sitting on a dangling bar instead of a basket, and then descend by parachute.

The balloon struck a tree and rolled against telephone wires. Adelaide's parachute was detached and fell upside down. It failed to right itself and Adelaide, as the *Peterborough Advertiser* on the 10th August declared: "falls like a wounded bird, 200 feet to the ground with a sickening thud". Death was inevitable.

Annie said the gasp from the crowd was so loud that she has never really forgotten it. This was a shocking experience for a five-year-old girl, and one which she never totally erased, as was evidenced in the way she told me the story eighty years later.

An inquest jury said that such exhibitions should be illegal, but that which came too late for the unfortunate Mademoiselle Bassett.

Mlle. Bassett, the unfortunate parachutist

Queen Victoria's Diamond Jubilee.

Two years later in June 1897, while Annie was at school, she took part in the celebrations for Queen Victoria's Diamond Jubilee. The Rectory Gardens in Peakirk was the venue for a party to celebrate the Queen's sixtieth anniversary. It

Diamond Jubilee celebrations for Queen Victoria 1897, Peakirk (above) and Crowland (below)

was a fine setting for a party, with elm trees and lush green grass. Union Jacks and colourful bunting were strewn all around the garden to heighten the scene, and all the local dignitaries were in attendance. More importantly, the weather was gloriously and appropriately hot. "We always used to say that whenever Queen Victoria had an important day, she was blessed with good weather" recalled Annie, who went on to win a bag of boiled sweets for winning a running race.

This was a time when all classes could come together to share in a mutual celebration. The Rector of Crowland Abbey, one of the local dignitaries, alluded at the jubilee service to the uplifting of the labouring classes and to the benefits of the spread of education. He said "the middle class might feel a great difficulty arising from the labouring classes having been raised to such power but they must still maintain their superiority". It was a time, then for everyone to celebrate without forgetting one's station!

The Jubilee was also given full treatment in Peterborough. A crowd of 6,000 children congregated in the Market Place for singing in the afternoon. These numbers were augmented by many other people later on, and in the words of the *Peterborough Advertiser* "the crowd stayed until the early hours of Wednesday morning, the town square echoing to the sounds of 'Rule Britannia'". The Mayor, John Thompson, gave a dinner to 550 workmen and friends at 'The Lindens'. Four hundred people took advantage of a free dinner for the aged at the Corn Exchange. A concert was also held at Peterborough Workhouse.

Sunday, Day of Worship

Sunday school was regarded as almost compulsory. They had been started in the 18th century to provide education to working class children. It was felt that the little ones would find the age-appropriate Bible teaching their young minds would absorb. Annie attended Sunday School at St Pega's Church, Peakirk and had to learn the Lord's Prayer and her catechism.

At about the same time, she went on a school trip to Deene Hall, Corby, the seat of the Brudenell family since 1514. The small school group travelled by horse-drawn wagon. This visit made a lasting impression, as she remembered that "Queen Elizabeth 1st had danced there and that there was no roof to the ballroom at that time." The current owner, Robert Brudenell, has, since 2014 continued the work of his parents who devoted their lives to the rehabilitation of the building.

Sunday was regarded as a special day – an important day. No one was supposed to work. It was a day of rest. When Annie was older, she used to play cards. She learned how to play Bridge. She said that she did feel a bit guilty doing this, though it seems quite innocuous today. Her very strict father, when a cousin came to visit, discovered that she was knitting. He said to her: "I would have thought that there were plenty of days in the week to do that". Sunday was a day for your best clothes and, of course, the obligatory hat. How times have changed!

Seaside Visit

In this same year of 1897 Annie remembers going to Hunstanton by train for a three-day holiday. She spent most of her time playing under the cliffs and jumping on stones from one to another. Simple pleasures indeed. You can see this exact area in the postcard below.

1038. Cliffs & Lighthouse, Hunstanton.

She also remembers having a large pole with which she kept her balance. There were the traditional donkeys, but she didn't have a ride. Hunstanton Pier, like many round the coast today, is a thing of the past, but she remembers that in 1897 not only was there a pier, but there was a concert too.

She had gone to 'Sunny Hunny' with her mother, Elizabeth, and a cousin. They travelled by charabanc, which was horse-drawn. She recalls that there were very few people there.

The postcard above is from 1900 and you can see a few people on the cliff top and a couple on the beach. It was only after the railway revolution of the 1840s and 1850s that people were really able to take holidays, but in the early days this usually precluded the working classes. Annie said that at holiday time, this really meant that people usually came to spend time with them, the Williams family, at the Decoy and these were family or friends.

The only other time she went to the seaside with her mother was in 1919 just after the war when they visited Skegness, which she didn't like very much: "The sea was far away." Something that might also have coloured her view of Skegness was the fact that there was a rail strike and she, and her mother, found great difficulty in getting home.

They spent a long time trying to get a charabanc that would get them somewhere near home. Eventually they found one that took them to Stamford, which was near, but not quite near enough. They managed to get a taxi which came from Peterborough to transport them back to the Decoy. The cost was a prohibitive and highly extortionate £5, which was a great deal for that time, but they just wanted to get home.

The Boer War

In 1900, while Annie was a pupil of Miss Pope in Lincoln Road East, she took part in what the local paper called "extraordinary scenes at Peterborough". This was the time of the Boer War and the town of Mafeking had just been relieved after a siege lasting 217 days. The *Advertiser* described the local scene in a style long dead: "about 10 o'clock at night, Peterborough was in its usual state of tranquillity and many had retired to rest. Then a triumphant yell 'Mafeking's relieved!' was borne on the night air and, if as by magic influence, the town centre was aroused to boisterous enthusiasm". This enthusiasm continued until midnight with groups of people cheering for the Queen, Baden-Powell, his army and General Buller. They waved Union Jacks, handkerchiefs and umbrellas. Martial songs like 'Soldiers of the Queen' were sung. The festivities continued the next morning at five o' clock with the sound of church bells, loco engines and small cannons. "Peterborough blossomed with flags as by a clever conjurer's trick" the newspaper reported.

Many schoolchildren were treated to an unforgettable sight. A great cannon from the Crimean War was fired at 3 pm, 4 pm and 5 pm. On this final occasion, an effigy of Paul Kruger, the Boer leader, was burned. The cannon was stuffed with Dutch cheese and fired at the burning effigy. The town became alive with fireworks, rockets, music and cheering and the crowd simply went berserk. The Relief of Mafeking (the lifting of the siege), while of little military significance, was a morale boost for the struggling British. This war marked the high tide of Britain's imperialist fever. Never again were her people to be so enthusiastic about their empire.

Annie, as a pupil of Miss Pope's school, joined in these festivities and firework displays. She was now ten years old and a knowing young woman. This time was regarded as a time for youth. Like many other schoolchildren at the time, she wore a button supporting one of the British generals in South Africa. These buttons were similar to those worn by American politicians and all of those on the periphery at election time. Annie's button supported the hard-pressed General Buller. She was able to recite part of a little rhyme that was popular at the time. It is testament to the education system then that she could recall the words nearly eighty years later:

> Lord Roberts, Kitchener, French, Buller and White
> All head of the army
> All ready to fight
> And when they catch Kruger…

Having said that she could not remember the rest, but it does help to give a picture of public opinion at that time.

The button that Annie wore, bearing Buller's image.

The Death of Queen Victoria

A small notice was pinned to the bulletin board at the gateway of Queen Victoria's Isle of Wight residence thus:

"Osborne House, January 22, 6.45pm
Her Majesty the Queen breathed her last at 6.30pm, surrounded by her children and grand-children."

The death of Queen Victoria heralded the end of an era. The nation was shocked to hear the news. Victoria, at age 81, had suffered an haemorrhagic stroke. The news broke almost immediately, and by the end of the following day most people had heard the shocking news. "My family had to go out and buy black hats." The nation was unprepared for a state funeral. Victoria had reigned for almost 64 years and nobody remembered the protocols.

An extract from the Lord Chamberlain's orders for 24th January, 1901 showed how the court was instructed to act:

"The ladies to wear black dresses trimmed with crepe, and black shoes and gloves and black furs, feathers and ornaments. The gentlemen to wear black court dress with black swords and buckles. The mourning to commence from the date of this order. The court to change the mourning on Wednesday 24th July next viz. Ladies to wear black dresses with coloured ribbons, flowers, feathers and ornaments. The gentlemen to continue the same mourning. And, on Friday 24th January next, the court is to go out of mourning."

This extract shows how much respect the nation was prepared to pay the late Queen.

Annie claimed that Victoria was regarded by many people as a goddess who was worshipped wherever she went. Many houses had a picture of the Queen displayed somewhere.

These, then, had been three massive events that became imprinted in Annie's mind at a young age

Annie's First Bicycle

It was at about this age (ten) that Annie got her first bicycle. "It was a posh affair – all chromium plated. It was a sort of status symbol because not many children had bikes then. It was difficult to ride in some places in the countryside, the Chase, for example, was far too bumpy. I remember penny farthing bicycles which would have been impossible to ride. It took me three weeks to learn and my father arranged a borrowed bike for me to learn on. I had problems balancing and kept on slipping off. Once I sat on the wheel and buckled it. Then, all of a sudden, I could do it. I could ride."

It was possible to cycle along Crowland Bank, but the roads really were awful. During the First World War granite was put down on the roads.

A few years later, when she was visiting friends who lived further in the Fens, she was stopped by the police. It was night time, so she needed the lights to be working on her bicycle. The problem was that Annie had no lights. Her friends had a spare rear light (red) so they affixed it to the bike – at the front. Along the route back she almost literally bumped into a policeman. With no small degree of sarcasm, he wondered why she wasn't riding backwards and, despite her fears ("we were all much more respectful of the Police in those days") he let her go with a stern warning. She then had a dynamo system of lights fitted to the bike, but was not particularly enamoured of them. "They were no good because when you stopped pedalling, the lights went out."

Health Matters

A less exciting first came in 1900 with Annie's first visit to a dentist, aged ten. She needed to have a tooth pulled and travelled into Peterborough. There was no anaesthetic but "lots of blood and pain and I kept the tooth as a souvenir. I remember gas being introduced which was not too expensive. The surgery was like today but not as sophisticated. The drill was never nice. All the houses kept tincture of cloves and laudanum. It is illegal now, but then it could be bought freely. It was used as a universal cure. Even if you cut yourself you used laudanum. I had cod liver oil when I was young and there were also liver pills and bile beans in the house.

Well before the days of the National Health Service, getting a doctor was a different and quite expensive experience. You did not have a special doctor as such but could go to anyone you liked. Of course, you had to pay for his services. "We often used both town (Peterborough) and country doctors. You paid separately for medicines and his fees." Lloyd George introduced a national health insurance scheme for low-paid working men in 1911. "The employer

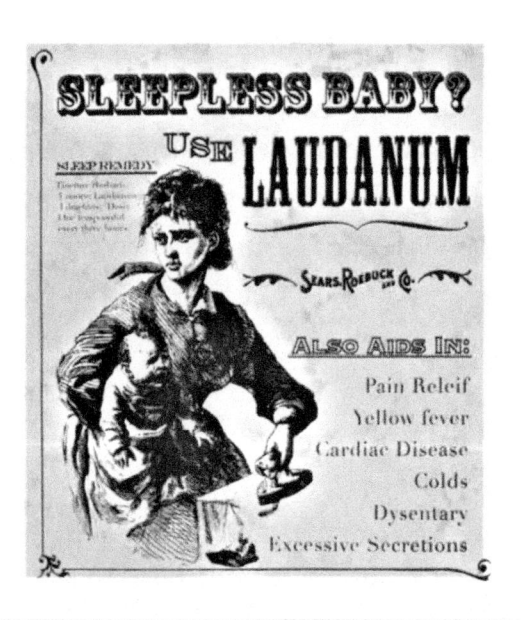

Advertisements for laudanum and Bile Beans, both with wonderfully exaggerated claims

paid some and you paid ten shillings a call. The workers had money deducted from their wages. This is how the labourers on the local farms and the Decoy were treated." This scheme ran until the Second World War, with the NHS starting in 1948.

Kettering High School

In 1902, Annie was sent to Kettering High School. The proprietress was an old lady whose three daughters helped with the teaching and the housekeeping. Besides the day girls – it was a single sex school – there were thirty boarders living in. The age range of the school was from twelve to eighteen years and the fees were about £40 per year, which was quite expensive for Edwardian England. The traditional Victorian ideals remained in vogue for social education. Girls were taught how to behave. In Annie's words they were being instructed "how to become snobs. We were told not to mix with common people". Young ladies then were not permitted to entertain views of a liberated nature. They were to be seen but not heard and to be quiet, well-mannered and passive. As we shall see, this was not the path that Annie wanted to progress down, especially as she grew older.

One of Annie's contemporaries, a girl called Maggie who was training to be a teacher, caused her to revise her ideas about working at school. Annie's teacher remarked, sarcastically, upon her achieving second place to Maggie in the regular weekly test. "I thought 'dash it all, I can beat Maggie any day'. I started to work hard then". Annie was soon able to put her words into practice and managed to relegate Maggie to second place behind her.

The subjects offered by Kettering High School were the traditional Maths, English, History, Geography, Religious Education and Art. English lessons were very formal with a lot of attention focused on grammar and compositions.

Annie was always good at writing. "You know Annie, I think that one day you will write books," her teacher told her. With characteristic humour she reflected "course I never did – I can't even write a letter now".

The foundations of Annie's lifelong interest in art and painting, however, were formulated during these early years at Kettering.

Studying the Bible and learning great passages by heart was educationally fashionable and Kettering was no exception to the rule. This took her back to her grandfather's daily morning prayers when she was younger. The church played a much more important role in society in those days before the Great War. Once a week the rector of the local parish came to the school to talk to the pupils and instruct them in the ways of the Lord. It was also customary practice for the boarders to take it in turn to play a hymn on the piano at night. Annie professed to being a poor piano player and said she always chose something simple like *Now The Day Is Over* "because it only had two verses". There was a peripatetic music teacher who came in to instruct the boarders in the art of keyboard playing which yielded mixed results.

Tennis was the main sport that was played – and that in clothing far removed from the frills that adorn centre court, Wimbledon today. Sport for ladies was still very refined and gentle, and no exertion was expected. Hockey, for example, was not on the syllabus. A popular recreation of the day was stilt walking. The pupils at Kettering spent many hours walking high on their stilts "and falling over" chuckled Annie.

There was no compulsory uniform. The girls were free

to wear what they wanted. Even though Edward VII was now King, fashion had not really changed and they still wore simple Victorian-style dresses. Some of the wealthier students used to go shopping on a Saturday morning. The fact that Kettering was a major shoe manufacturing area meant that leather boots were a favourite item.

Annie shared a bedroom with three other girls, two of them daughters of Thorney farmers. She was the youngest of the group and always reckoned to be the naughty one, even though she wasn't. She remembers being sent to bed early once over some incident which she cannot recall. She said that she saw her role as the "clown" of the group and her endeavours to make the others laugh were often misinterpreted by those in authority.

A shilling a week was spent on fruit and sweets. You had to keep an account of what you had spent so that it could later be scrutinized by a teacher. This was supposed to teach you how to manage your financial affairs.

The food served at Kettering at meal times was of a high standard, unlike that of the Lincoln Road East dame school. Their 'speciality of the house' was boiled rice in a bag, which was considered a dry, tasteless meal. At Kettering, Annie had an ally in a parlour maid called Bailey. She always kept a look out for Annie's Oliver-like plea of "can I have some more?" when it came to meal times. Bailey could be relied upon to provide a good second helping.

Life at Kettering was pleasant, but for Annie it was far from this on a Friday evening. This was the night when hair was washed. Annie had long, thick hair which took a long time to dry. Of course, there were no hair dryers at that time, which meant that she had to suffer what seemed like hours of hard towel rubbing. This often led to a mass of tangled hair which then had to be painfully combed out.

A dance instructor travelled from London to the school to teach the girls: The Lancers, the Quadrille, the Polka, the Valeta and the Barn Dance were among Annie's favourites. "We had social evenings at school but they weren't so much fun with only girls." At the official dance class sessions there were boys present, but they were young and small. "We used to frown at them to make them go away if they came up and asked you to dance."

The age of the chaperone was rapidly dying out. After leaving school, Annie would go to the Angel Hotel in Peterborough, where they held tea dances in the afternoon. "Much older men used to come to these. Goodness knows where they found the time during the day."

Annie left Kettering at the age of fifteen. "I got fed up with writing" she confessed, "so I left". She sent her parents a letter announcing "I am leaving at the end of this term. If you don't send my notice, I shan't come back". And so she returned home. There was no pressure on a career for girls in those days. As you had to pay for your own education, nobody really bothered much about early leaving. Your life was your own.

Back home

When she left school, aged fifteen, she became involved with helping in the family poultry business. Cockerels were sent to London by train and ducks from the Decoy were also sent from Peakirk railway station. London prices for the poultry were about 7/6d each. A poultry man used to come to the decoy and buy the birds for 2/6d or 3/-. Eggs were also sold to Peterborough shops via a local egg collector – a woman who bought them from Annie's mother. This business really began to grow in the years just before the Great War.

Annie, who was now looking for money for her little bit of independence, said "I used to get a very small share of what the poultry was sold for", but it was never enough. "It was like digging gold out of my mother and father to get a shilling or two, pocket money! My parents didn't want to pay me for my work at this time. They did give me money for clothes. They were waiting to see me married off. If I had two or three shillings in my purse then I had to consider myself well off."

Another of the seemingly exciting events in Annie's formative years was the still vivid memory of seeing her first ever motor car while at Kettering. She describes the scene in the following way: "There was a cloud of dust about a mile away down the road. The word went round, 'car coming! car coming!' A great noisy vehicle thundered past us. We were all frightened and jumped into the hedge as it approached".

Peterborough Agricultural Show

Farming and the countryside were always at the core of Annie's life. Peterborough Agricultural Show was an event she first attended at the age of ten in 1900. It was held at Millfield, on a site behind the Windmill Inn, Windmill Street. It was quite a small affair, but important nonetheless. "The women went in landaus, all very smartly dressed. I remember the parade of animals and the firework display at night. We used to grow delphiniums and sweet peas at the Decoy and the soil was very rich. I used to enter the flower competitions at Millfield and won first prize for my delphiniums one year."

"We used to go every year, especially after it moved to Eastfield (1911) which was a much bigger site. I saw Edward VII, George VI and the Queen Mother one year. Princess Alice, the Duchess of Gloucester, was a regular visitor too. It was always a very smart affair. The ladies wore wonderful frocks and hats – it was like Royal Ascot. After the war people could not be bothered to maintain the smartness. I have been to the Alwalton site, where it moved again (in 1968), but it has become far too big. You can't often find what you want. I was only interested in the flower tent." Annie's favourite subject for her paintings, her flowers, had lasted all of this time.

King Edward VII and Queen Consort Alexandra
George V and Queen Mary???????

Annie's verdict on the new King, Edward VII, from pursed lips, was that was "he was a bit of a gay lad" ('gay' used in its original meaning of 'light-hearted and carefree', of course.) It was clear that she was not enamoured. He only reigned for ten years and never commanded the sort of respect that her beloved Victoria had.

Alexandra continued the public side of her life, devoting time to her charitable causes and setting one up in 1913 after the death of her husband. One such cause was Alexandra Rose Day, when artificial roses made by people with disabilities were sold in aid of hospitals by women volunteers. The charity was set up to mark the 50th anniversary of Alexandra's arrival in Britain. Annie was involved one year in travelling to London to help sell the artificial roses.

When Edward had died in 1910 no one had really heard the news, a completely different scenario from when Queen Victoria had died. "We heard that Alexandra permitted Edward's long-standing mistress to visit the king as he lay dying. We respected her for that."

The people at the Decoy found out from a passing man who said that the king had died. "We asked him how he knew and he said that he had been working near Willow Drove when a man rode past on a bicycle and told him. That's how the news got to Peakirk".

This postcard, from the time, is wishing a prosperous reign to 'Our Sailor King'. Some of the names above: Mr Palmer (St. Guthlac); E. Fillingham (Neptune); J. Truman (John Bull); Nelson's Navy (R. White) The Empire Overseas (Mr Goodwin) Peace (Miss Goodwin) and Britannia (Annie Williams herself)

Annie recalls taking part in the above celebration in Crowland to herald the coronation of George V on 22nd June 1911. She took part on one of twelve horse drawn floats in the parade. Each float had a separate theme, and Annie's float represented the four nations of Great Britain. She was thrilled to play the part of Britannia.

"I had to hire the costume, which cost thirty shillings – a lot of money for that time. The breastplate was all gold coins". Who would seriously turn down that role in a nation where patriotism, jingoism and nationalism were still very much paramount?

Annie's family were committed monarchy supporters. She recalls that the man who was destined to become her husband nine years later stood by the horse in the picture. The venue for this celebration was Snowden's Field. The parade had assembled in Abbey Square, Crowland, and from there progressed to the field. The square was crowded, with many people on horseback. There was a brass band playing in the evening for dancing. The celebration closed with a big firework display. The cost of the whole event was £100, which came out of the local rates.

Annie admired George V, especially after the much-publicised lifestyle of the previous King. George looked stern, but she admired him. "Our family always thought a lot about the Royal family. We were good monarchists. We liked Queen Mary too, but she was not like our Alexandra". There was great patriotism, especially when war did break out. Thousands rushed to join up. "It will be all over by Christmas!"

Annie with the expensive gold coin breastplate

Before the Great War, Annie saw her very first aeroplane. It had reputedly flown in from France, though not piloted by Louis Blériot (who was the first to fly across the Channel in 1909) as had been widely, erroneously touted. It was due to land somewhere near Marholm. The time given for its arrival was 6 pm. There were very many ponies and traps brimming with expectant crowds who waited, and waited - and waited. Nothing happened. Was it a hoax? In fact something had gone wrong earlier on and it had been forced down at St. Neots and was not capable of flying again till the next day. The pilot flew from St. Neots to Peterborough, covering the 37 miles in 28 minutes at a height of 2,000 feet. "We all went again the next day and this time, we were able to see an aeroplane land with just one man in it." The man was W.H. Ewen, a Scottish aviator and, actually only the sixty-third person to hold the Aviator's Certificate in Britain. He was the first man to land a plane in Peterborough. A pioneer indeed.

The landing place was given as Walton, this time in a field owned by Mr. A Hunt. The crowds had gathered to see this man-made bird at close quarters and the cheers grew

Mr. William Hugh Ewen and Annie's "frail-looking plane"

louder and louder as the small speck in the sky grew bigger as it neared the landing spot. Annie thought the biplane was "a frail-looking plane" but she was still excited to witness it at first hand.

Ewen was presented with a silver rose bowl to mark the historic occasion, which had been paid for by a number of local businessmen. He stayed the night at a house belonging to the Brown family on Marholm Road. "He would have been all right – the family had a lot of daughters," Annie

said with a mischievous grin. She stayed the two nights so that she wouldn't miss anything. I don't know if she is in this picture of the crowd that had gathered, but it is likely, given that she vowed not to miss a thing.

This is not the end of the story, because there was more drama after Mr. Ewen had given a series of displays over the weekend. A large crowd gathered to watch him take off for Lincoln early on Monday morning. He almost hit a large tree at Marholm Woods. The crowd thought that he would crash, but Ewen had the biplane under control. He looked to land, and it came down gracefully until well within the reach of the earth, but then it dropped rapidly and failed to land on the skids. The engine dug into the ground and one of the shafts of the propeller was broken off and part of the under chassis was broken. A messy end to an historic and dramatic event, but Ewen was unscathed.

He served in the Royal Flying Corps and Royal Air Force during the Great War, reaching the rank of Major, resigning his commission due to ill health in 1918. He died in 1947. A largely unsung hero.

Special Celebrations

This was an era when a number of festivals or special days were held each year. Just before Christmas, on St Thomas's Day 21st December, the widows from the parish came round begging for money. "This was called Gooding and was a well-recognised custom."

We are not daily beggars
That beg from door to door
But we are neighbours' children
Whom you have seen before.

This carol did try to show that this was not out and out begging, but fellow folk who had fallen on hard times.

Plough Monday followed on 6th January (or the nearest Monday to that date) It signified the end of the midwinter holiday break and is related to fertility. It also played up the part the humble ploughman would have had in a predominantly very agricultural setting. "A boy would come round with his face all blackened up, offering to dance in return for money for local landowners." Certainly not the done thing today!

A big festive custom was May Day. "We put up lots of garlands up to decorate the Decoy. People used to come from near and far to help with the decorating. A lot came from Newborough. It started very early in the morning. It was like a race to see who would get there first with their garlands and bunting. We gave the first ones half a crown and the last ones got sixpence!"

In an age today where fireworks on 5th November are virtually all big events rather than the back garden private celebrations from years ago, I was a little surprised when Annie said that they did not celebrate Guy Fawkes in the village "No one could afford the fireworks." When there were many traditional events celebrated, it seemed strange that this one was missed out.

Crowland Floods, 1912/13

1912 and 1913 saw the Crowland and Peakirk area flooded, in common with other fenland areas. Annie obviously remembered them, as she did the 1947 floods where she took an active role. More on this later. As shown in the postcard below, the harvest fields were flooded. The water came from the Nine Bridges and Northborough direction, leaving most of Peakirk under water as well as the harvest fields in Crowland. Many farmers lost their harvest and sadly, unlike the later 1947 event, there was no compensation. Will's family farm in Crowland was very lucky. Unlike others, it suffered a minimal loss.

Chapter 4

THE WAR YEARS

The Great War, 1914-18

Annie used to go to dances with her friends, which was a good way to meet people. She got engaged in 1910 (aged 20), to a naval officer. The engagement did not last "as he was an alcoholic".

With her friends Nellie and Annie Bodger, she used to go cycling every night. It was a very popular pastime and "the only thing you really did" confessed Annie. They would cycle to Market Deeping and back and hardly ever bothered about having lights on their bikes.

This was her social life until war broke out in 1914. "It was a shock to us. I don't think that any of us really expected it". It suddenly happened on 4th August. "We had heard about Serbia and the Archduke, but hadn't realised that it mattered to us. We didn't get daily newspapers but received them by post – a day late".

Britain, led by Prime Minister Herbert Asquith, had given Germany an ultimatum to get out of Belgium by midnight of August 3rd 1914. This did not happen, and war was declared on the very next day, the 4th.

"Although I was surprised when it actually broke out, I think that deep down I always knew we were going to fight with Germany. My friend the naval officer had told me before that the Navy expected such a thing. It had something to do with the building of Dreadnaughts". Annie said that she had had a dream before the war. "I saw all these Germans marching along Crowland Bank towards our way and then I saw something that startled me. The sky was full of parachutes. It was all pretty colours and they were dropping from the sky. On the parachutes there was written 'Remember the 5th of May next year", but nothing happened on that date." This vivid dream obviously made a lasting impression on Annie.

Once the nationalistic fervour had died down, the impact of the war was soon to takes its toll. Most people were short of food as things progressed, because so much was sent to the soldiers at the front. Rationing was finally introduced in 1918. Sugar, meat, flour, butter, margarine and milk were all rationed so that everyone got what they needed. Each person had special ration cards, even King George and Queen Mary.

Examples of rationing:

Butter 2oz (50g), Sugar 8oz (225g), Cheese 2oz (50g), Jam 1lb (450g) every two months, Bacon and ham 4oz (100g), Meat to the value of 1s 2d (6p today), Eggs 1 fresh egg per week, Dried eggs 1 packet every four weeks

As farming folk, the Williams family found that this hardly affected them - they had a pig. There were always wild ducks to eat, and pheasant and chickens. Annie's father, Herbert, was general farming at that time so there was wheat, potatoes and mangels as well as the sheep and cows.

Annie used to assist with the feeding of the lambs and calves. The Government issued instructions as to what crops to grow if you didn't already grow them. Annie said that they "used to get round it as it was a silly waste of time". Herbert was still catching ducks at the decoy and Annie used to assist him. She said her father was an expert in killing the birds. There would be mallards, teal, wigeon and shovelers. "Father used to lock the wings and twist the necks – he could kill hundreds in a very short time." This probably sounds cruel but was regarded as more humane than shooting them.

Food prices rose during the war. The Williams family "did all right" to use the vernacular. Annie laughed as she recounted that "there was a silly thing with sugar rationing. If you had fruit trees you were allowed so many pounds per tree. If you counted up your currants and gooseberry bushes you could have had tons of sugar". Billy charged more for chickens to those who wanted them. "Oh yes, we made quite a lot of money during the first war."

There was an incident in Peterborough that got almost everyone talking. It was difficult not to have a view. Two days after war was declared, Mr Frederick Frank, a pork butcher of German extraction but a long-term resident of Peterborough, and a hitherto well-respected man, had his shop smashed by a crowd of over 500 people. The yeomanry was called in to drive the crowd back. Frank's home, too, was showered with bricks. The upshot of this was twenty-four men being charged with various offences – some were imprisoned, some were fined and four accepted conscription to the war. Annie, who knew the shop, offered sadly, "How fickle are people?"

Many of the local lads went off to fight. Conscription was introduced in 1916 via the Military Service Act in January. The act specified that single men aged 18 to 40 years old were liable to be called up for military service unless they were widowed with children or ministers of a religion. Billy Williams was called up. Recruits were sorted into three classes, A, B, and C, in order of fitness for front-line service. In 1918, 75 per cent were classed as "A", some "B" men also had to be sent into the trenches. "B" was for the artillery and the final class "C" was for work behind the lines. Because of an injury to Billy's toe in Canada, described below, he was classed as C3. He was actively called up from 1916, but didn't leave these shores until 1917. He remained in Mesopotamia for three years and had no leave at all. This was the reason that Annie and Billy were not able to get married until he was finally able to return in early 1920.

Annie was very critical of David Lloyd-George, who became Prime Minister in 1916: "He was a Liberal and we were Conservatives. I liked Winston Churchill, who was First Lord of the Admiralty. He sent the fleet out at the Battle of Jutland. The naval officer I had been engaged to did not like Churchill. He said he was too strict. He had too many rules."

I mentioned the ill-fated Gallipoli campaign, for which Churchill shouldered a lot of the blame, and she did concede that there was "a terrible waste of life". She told me that the local Rector's son, Frances Faithfull, had joined up and was killed within four weeks of reaching the front at the Second Battle of Ypres, 1915. He was just eighteen years old. If you were a 2nd Lieutenant, you were the first over the top in the trenches and therefore one of the very first German targets. "They didn't have a chance. Nobody had expected this kind of warfare". It had been the era of the cavalry charges.

Peakirk and the War

The Rector, the Reverend Faithfull, donated the land for the building of the Village Hall in Peakirk in his son's memory. Francis, the son, is pictured below. War memorials were being erected across the nation to honour those who have fallen as a result of war or conflict. The Peakirk Roll of Honour has photographs and details of not only those who died, but all who served from the village. This one has details of their service history including the aforementioned, eighteen-year-old Francis W.A. Faithfull.

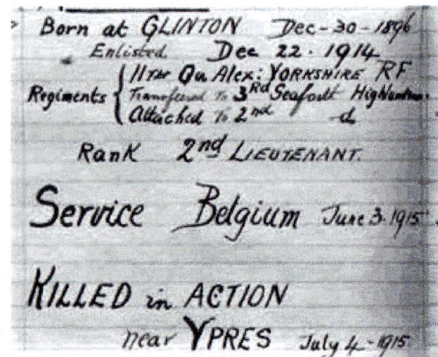

Curiously, the monument in the centre of Peakirk is not a war memorial. It was commissioned a full ten years before the First World War by The Reverend Edward James, who was a curate and then the parish priest from 1853 until 1912, and was erected to commemorate his 50th anniversary in 1903. The only inscription on the monument is "E.J. 1904".

Wartime Nurse

"I went to Charing Cross Hospital in London as a nurse in November 1914." Annie, however, did not like the job. "It was very hard work. Nurses in those days were like charwomen. It was scrubbing and cleaning everywhere. We had to go round with the doctors and help with dressings. We washed patients and gave them food. We started at 7 am every day and were allowed two hours off in total during the long shifts."

The Peakirk monument at the centre of the village

Annie was at Charing Cross over Christmas and did not go home at all. While she was working there Herbert Asquith, the Prime Minister, came to visit patients, as did the Secretary of State for War, Richard Haldane, who had implemented major changes to the Army after the experiences of the two Boer Wars at the turn of the century. "The best bit about Christmas was going round the wards singing carols with the choir from St Martin's in the Field".

While at Charing Cross, Annie stayed in the Nurses' Home. She didn't get paid because it was a training college. "I stayed in my own room and it was quite comfortable. The food was very good... and didn't we used to eat." Food was prepared in a dining area at the basement block of the hospital. "We worked so hard that it made us hungry". In the two hours' break that they were allotted she went for walks with fellow trainee nurses. "We couldn't go very far within the two hours but we used to go to the Haymarket and Regent Street. London was a very busy place, especially for one who was used to living in the countryside. There always seemed to be lots of cars and buses everywhere. All night long you could hear the noises of taxis and cars".

A contributory reason for Annie rushing off to be a nurse was the break-up of her engagement to her naval officer friend. She was upset and needed a complete break. "I needed a change of environment, and despite the very hard work it certainly pulled me together".

Home

I have already mentioned how Annie had got involved with

the family poultry business. She quit the nursing job at the end of January, 1915 and returned home again to the chickens and ducks. The sights she had endured at Charing Cross certainly contributed to this. "We guessed that it was not going to be the short war that had been predicted. I couldn't see it ever ending". Newspapers with exaggerated stories of German atrocities in Belgium and the horrific injuries she witnessed on the wards meant that Annie had just had enough. Though she left before the casualties of the poison gas attacks came in, she certainly needed to change her environment yet again.

Enter Billy Williams

When Annie came back from working in the hospital in London, she planned to marry Will Williams. We need to learn a little about Will, or Billy, in the days before that marriage. He was born in 1882 and lived in Crowland, and his father was a baker and confectioner. He joined his father's business, but as times were hard, he sought adventure and took advantage of a government scheme which saw him emigrate and settle in Canada. This was partly enabled by the fact that his elder brother, Edward, had moved there a few years before.

In Saskatchewan, Billy worked on a 160-acre ranch. Life was hard and the winters long and very cold. At this time of year, he would seek employment in the many lumber camps. Here he suffered a very nasty accident when an axe handle slipped and he struck his foot, almost completely severing his toes. Some of his fellow lumbermen suggested he should go off immediately to the hospital, but that was 40 miles away. An old half-caste French Canadian Indian trapper said "You go to hospital, you lose your money, you lose your toes. Stay with Francois, you save your money, you save your toes."

Billy stayed and was treated by the trapper with a concoction of birch bark and sphagnum moss. His wounds did eventually heal, although he was left with a very stiff forefoot. This did cause a very fit man to be later graded C3 when he went before a medical board during the Great War. He was not called up until 1917. After a few failed Canadian crop harvests, he decided to return to Britain, where he joined another brother who had set up as a pea, corn and produce merchant back in Crowland. This was a more prosperous venture.

Billy served in Mesopotamia (modern Iraq) for the three years, not returning until February 1920. There were still wars going on with the Kurds and the Arabs. He was in the Army Service Corps (ASC). During the First World War, the (ASC) operated the transport systems that delivered ammunition, food and equipment to the Front Line. It used motor vehicles, the railways and waterways as part of a complex supply line linking Britain to the various Fronts.

These men were the unsung heroes of the conflict. They travelled by lorry in 1917 from France to the bottom of Italy and thence by ship. They crept around the coast because of German U-boats, past Greece and into the Red Sea at the hottest time of the year (August). Annie recalls how Billy told her that drinking water was very low, but on the upper decks the officers drank whisky with ice. When they finished their drinks, they would throw the ice cubes to the deck below. The thirsty troops then scrabbled around trying to scoop up the melting ice. Many of them just used to lie down on the deck in the shade, if they could, as it was so hot. Some even died before they arrived at their destination. Once they finally arrived there, close to Basra, they discovered that there was little or no food arranged for them.

The Gallipoli campaign on 1915 was widely, and almost certainly correctly, criticised for a lack of planning. (see comment above). Just two years later it seemed that no lessons had been learned at all. The conditions had not been properly assessed or acted upon.

Billy used to write letters from the Middle East, and they took about two months to arrive. Naturally they were censored." If they came in a green envelope they had been censored, but a blue envelope meant that the officers had not censored the contents. I can't believe they actually read every single line of every single letter," she said.

Soldiers were not permitted to mention where they were or about any possible manoeuvres. "Will used to put one letter (of the alphabet) on one page, and one on the next and so on, so that when I put all the letters together, I could work out where he was" she confided. Echoes of Mata Hari here!

Billy was in Mesopotamia for almost three years and during that time, he spent a long period in hospital. Sandfly fever was quite prevalent. He went out one day with a fellow soldier in an armoured car; they had heard that there were hostile tribes around. He looked up and saw that there were hordes of men in flowing robes on the horizon. He didn't know what to do but grabbed a hand grenade, prepared it and advanced towards the enemy. When the armoured car reached its destination there was not a single mark in the sand. It had been a mirage, and a sign that he was not at all well. The stereotypical example of this condition is for a thirsty man to see an oasis in the middle of the desert which turns out not to be there. Billy's mirage was a step beyond this, hence the hospitalisation. It was, in fact, a serious case of malaria, a disease which would blight him, on and off, for the rest of his life.

Service in Mesopotamia at that time was not much fun, to put it mildly. Annie told how Billy would be affected by bouts of malaria for up to seven years. Within this time frame he might be all dressed up and ready to go out somewhere when he would suddenly start shivering with a high fever, become delirious and have to be put to bed, wrapped in blankets. He would be given quinine and lime juice and made to stay in bed. His pyjamas would be wringing wet and have to be constantly changed. Suddenly after four days, before his strength had fully returned, he might feel better, but he still needed to take things easy. The thing about this disease was that there was little warning when it might reappear. It was sporadic, but you never knew when I would hit.

According to the Battalion's account in the 1920 Rifle Brigade Chronicle, 'the weather and temperature dominated the situation, 60F degrees variation between dawn and midday was common' with the maximum temperature under canvas reaching 125F degrees in August and the minimum in November falling to 20F degrees.

Each company was given a sheep per day for food. "It was so thin that when you hung it up, it was like a lantern. You could see right through it. Billy took over the role of cook for his company and became quite good at it. He would boil the sheep with pearl barley and any other vegetable he could lay his hands on.

The soldiers did have a glass of whisky occasionally. The Sergeant Major in their company of the Seaforth Highlanders was a Freemason and somehow managed to obtain it from time to time. Billy became friendly with him and was often given a bottle of the prized whisky by the Sergeant Major. He shared this with his fellow soldiers.

He was recommended to go for officer training, but always rejected it. He wanted to stay with his mates. The camaraderie was good. His role was to serve behind enemy lines and not active combat. A major part of his duties concerned the maintenance and repair of the Light Armoured Motor Battery Car. The following is a picture of such a vehicle.

Billy saw action one day in an unexpected way. A fellow soldier, a Gurkha, ran up to him and shouted "Look, Turks!" A large group of enemy Turkish soldiers had marched smartly into the British camp to give themselves up. Billy was branded as a hero for a while for this event – capturing all the enemy troops.

While serving in the land between the Tigris and the Euphrates rivers and thus Babylon, Will did get the opportunity, in his leisure time, to visit a number of ancient tombs and sites. He even brought a piece of the Tower of Babel back home after visiting the ruins in Babylon. He said the highlight of this cultural sightseeing was to visit the tomb of Nebuchadnezzar, a name he knew from the Bible.

The journey out to Mesopotamia had been a difficult passage, but the journey home was equally challenging. There were no boats to take them home. They came home via Bombay, in India, a long way round, to land at Liverpool on 11 February 1920. The soldiers were all thin and frail and stood in swaying lines upon return to British soil. He was then happily demobilised.

Billy had been serving in the Middle East when Armistice Day came on 11th November 1918 and it was not properly celebrated. Annie was at the Decoy with her parents. "Colonel Imre came round to tell us that the war was over. With Will away it was difficult to celebrate fully".

There were local celebrations and street parties. In Crowland the bells clanged and crowds of people 'made merry as they felt' to quote a local newspaper. A united thanksgiving was held in the evening in the Wesleyan Chapel. Later in the evening, as in most towns and villages in the country, the young folk danced and lit bonfires in the street in celebration. A few miles away Annie, whose Will was serving overseas told me, "but we did not join in. We were happy, but we could not celebrate till Will came home".

Chapter 5

BACK HOME

Rook Shooting

Annie had just started going out with Billy when he took her out along the Crowland Bank to a place where there was a rookery. Rooks were regarded as pests and when numbers were high a shoot was organised. "I had never been shooting before. They showed me how to use the sights on the gun and I got 22. It was as easy as anything. I didn't go again. I didn't much like it." Apparently, the advice she was given, which does sound cruel, hence her dislike of the event, was to shoot the young ones which wouldn't stay in the nest but were not old enough to be able to fly properly.

Rook pie just uses the breasts of these birds, and some recipes of the day called for hard-boiled eggs to be put with them for extra taste. "Some people used to eat sparrows, especially when times were hard and they were hungry".

> **1323.—ROOK PIE.**
>
> **Ingredients.**—6 young rooks, ¾ of a lb. of rump steak, ¼ of a lb. of butter, ½ a pint of stock, salt and pepper, paste.
>
> **Method.**—Skin the birds without plucking them, by cutting the skin near the thighs, and drawing it over the body and head. Draw the birds in the usual manner, remove the necks and backs, and split the birds down the breast. Arrange them in a deep pie-dish, cover each breast with thin strips of steak, season well with salt and pepper, intersperse small pieces of butter, and add as much stock as will ¾ fill the dish. Cover with paste (see Veal Pie), and bake from 1½ to 2 hours, for the first ¼ hour in a hot oven to make the paste rise, and afterwards more slowly to allow the birds to become thoroughly cooked. When the pie is about ¾ baked, brush it over with yolk of egg to glaze the crust, and, before serving, pour in, through the hole on the top, the remainder of the stock.
>
> **Time.**—To bake, from 1½ to 2 hours. **Average Cost,** uncertain, as they are seldom sold. **Sufficient** for 5 or 6 persons.
>
> THE ROOKS are wild birds, found abundantly in most parts of Britain and Ireland. They live in communities, and feed on seeds, insects and vermin. Their flesh is tough and coarse-flavoured. Only the young birds are eaten, generally being shot almost before they take to the wing. The backbones and adjoining flesh is always removed, as these parts have a strong, bitter taste, which soon contaminates the rest of the flesh.

The recipe for rook pie from Mrs Beeton's Household Management Book

This seems an appropriate place to mention another animal which was anathema to the farming community – the fox. The Fitzwilliam Hunt was a well- known and widely supported body. The notion of fox hunting in the early days of the twentieth century was not regarded as a problem. "Foxes used to get down in the Decoy after the ducks. We had to shut the poultry up. One night a fox got in. I heard the noise through my bedroom window. I took the three dogs and went downstairs in my nightdress. We chased the fox, who had taken a hen. As the dogs got nearer the fox dropped the hen and ran off. I picked her up and she was OK apart from a few teeth marks on her back. We used to set traps for the foxes.

"One spring, after the ducks had gone, we held a shoot. We killed five foxes that year in one shoot. Peter Scott was one of the hunters. One of the other hunters was a man called Baxter, who was in the potato business, but could not shoot at all. His gun went off accidentally and he peppered a number of his fellow shooters. Peter Scott threw himself to the ground, as the gun was aimed straight at him. One of Peter's friends, Christopher Dalgetty, was part of the hunting party. Baxter went up to him and asked if he could borrow some cartridges. Dalgetty said 'No, certainly not! I am not going to get shot by one of my own cartridges'. There was always a meal and a drink after the shoot and Baxter could not understand why no one would talk to him.

"We used to host two or three pheasant shoots a year, which were very popular. Hare coursing was done anywhere and I remember one event a big one held at nearby Postland. The River Welland was not very wide then and a lot of the men would go fishing at Crowland. The river widened after the '47 floods."

The Postwar Era

Although there was little unemployment in the Crowland and Peakirk area – farmers did prosper – Annie was aware that the many returning soldiers had a very difficult time. "Many became beggars, playing instruments for money. They had a hard time readjusting to life". She did say that at the end of the war she hoped that the Kaiser would be killed. "We were very bloodthirsty." Stories of German atrocities in Belgium were still being believed, and they felt that "the Germans were not badly treated after the war with the peace treaty".

Although they had not properly celebrated the Armistice, it was a different story in 1919 for the Peace Celebrations on 19th July. Annie had a friend who lived in Twickenham and had spent time with her on the river. Her friend had a dinghy and they used to go to Eel Pie Island. She and the friend went to the celebrations together. "There were thousands of people. We got a place near Albert Gate, which was not a good viewpoint but there it was! We missed the Navy go past. We were sitting on the kerb when Douglas Haig, on horseback, came charging across the park. He jumped his horse right over where we were sitting, which caused us to shout out loud. Apparently, he was trying to join the parade and taking a short cut. We got a great view of that!" There were 15,000 troops in the parade.

Douglas Haig on his horse, having caught up with the parade

Annie was also with an aunt and two cousins, one of whom was deaf. At the end the crowd just milled about and "we got parted. I was stranded with the cousin who was deaf. We were stuck in the park for a long time going absolutely nowhere. We were forced to go with the flow – where the stream of bodies went.

There were lots of fireworks, which added to the chaos. "We hadn't the time to appreciate them. We eventually managed to get onto a bus. I knew where we were supposed to be going but did not know where the bus was headed. It was so crowded. My deaf cousin was pushed off the bus and I was pushed upstairs. I didn't think my cousin was on the bus at all. It was about 3 am. The buses always used to run all night in London in those days. I asked the woman next to me where the bus was going and if she knew where the address we had to find was. Luckily, we were on the right bus and the woman told me which stop to get off and how to walk to our destination. As I got off the bus, I noticed my cousin, who was sat huddled up. She had been pushed back on. We then walked to our destination and actually arrived well before the other two."

Annie and Billy Get Married

Less than two months after Billy's return, on 5th April 1920, there was a wedding at Peakirk Church (St Pega's) – a small one. Billy was quite shy and said "Let's get married early in the morning – there won't be anyone in the church". Annie told him she could not get ready before 10.30 am, exercising her woman's prerogative. The taxi to pick her up arrived at the house half an hour late. They then had had problems cranking the engine up to start it. The woman who had come to help with the veil, and her husband, had to give the car a tow in order to get it started. They got halfway down the Chase when one of the bridesmaids realised that she left the bouquet behind. The car could not turn round, so she had to run back to fetch it. This made them later still.

The Wedding March had been played twice before they arrived, due to false alarms. The priest had gone to sleep, and when they were finally ready he had to be prodded to rouse him. By now the church was crowded with people, not at all how Billy had envisioned things. He must have been very relieved when the ceremony was finally concluded successfully.

The reception was, as Billy had hoped, a small affair. With Annie and a few members of family and friends they went out for a meal before heading on a mystery tour. They hadn't really planned a honeymoon and in their Bullnose Morris car they headed south. The first stop was in Cambridge, where they spent two nights at the University Arms in the centre of the city. This hotel is still flourishing today and is regarded as one of the very best.

Someone had told them that Lynton in Devon was "a nice place", so they set off there. They arrived in Oxford and left the car there before journeying by train to Weymouth. They didn't like the look of this town, so they took a train and a charabanc to Lynton. The newly-weds were the only passengers on the vehicle. "The driver took a short

A motorised charabanc (1920s). This superseded the horse-drawn version and was in turn soon to be overtaken by buses as the main form of people carrier.

cut down Porlock Hill, which was a one in three gradient. I tied my bonnet back and the driver cut the engine and then we coasted downhill at a fair old rate of knots."

The happy couple stayed for a few days in Porlock Hill in a "pretty little thatched cottage" which was nearby. They made their way back to the Decoy gradually and ended up living at Annie's parent's house. It was a big house and there was plenty of room.

Life with Mr and Mrs Herbert Williams was not difficult. Billy had no experience at all of work in a decoy but, being a man with an enquiring mind and interested in all aspects of nature, he soon gained the necessary expertise in all the maintenance work that was required. His experience of life in Canada had in some way helped to prepare him for what was to become his future occupation. When his father-in-law died in 1929, Billy was easily capable of taking over the running of the whole enterprise

European ventures

In 1922, Annie and Billy went to Boulogne for a day. They stayed with friends in Folkestone before crossing the Channel by ferry the next morning. They had few holidays, as they were fully occupied at the Decoy. Herbert was still overseeing things, which did afford a little time now and again to get away. The norm was friends and family visiting them at home. They had lots of visitors who came to see the birds and wildlife in general. The Headmaster of Oundle Public School came to visit with his son James, who later became a friend of Peter Scott – but more of that later.

Another European trip saw Annie visit Germany shortly after the war. She went with her bridesmaid, Dorothy Palmer. It was a package tour with Lunn's Tours and they took a ferry to Ostend, a coach to Brussels and from there into Germany. They journeyed down the River Rhine to Cologne and then Bonn, where they stayed. Part of their party was heading south to the Black Forest, but they stayed at a very prestigious hotel frequented by millionaires and the jet set. "We joined up with a group from London. We were sort of millionaires in those days. There was an orchestra at the hotel and it played requests for us on the terrace, where we all danced." Annie's knack of being somewhere important at the right time was demonstrated on this tour as well.

Hyperinflation was plaguing Germany. The Weimar Republic which governed the country in the post-war era had huge financial problems and Annie witnessed the results first-hand. Hyperinflation caused money to be virtually worthless and overprinted several times, so that for example a loaf of bread that cost 163 marks in 1921 cost 1,500,000 marks by September 1923, and at the peak of hyperinflation, in November 1923, it had reached the 200,000,000,000 mark. The British visitors felt little sympathy for this until Annie talked to some German people at a Bonn night club who told her of the attrition they had suffered during the war. Annie was aware that Britain had suffered from the German U-boats sinking ships carrying provisions for Britain but hadn't realised that the ordinary German citizens suffered food shortages as well, due to Allied blockades.

Annie told me, as a die-hard Conservative supporter all of her life, that news of the Russian Revolution and the deaths of the Romanov Royal Family horrified her. The fact that Russia had initially fought on the same side as Britain and France was muddled when the communists took over and Russia surrendered to the Germans. "There was no real fear of a Communist revolution in Britain" she said. However, both she and Billy had no time for the Labour Party. "Will despised the Labour Party and Ramsay McDonald, who became Prime Minister [briefly in 1924 and again 1929-31]. We used to feel sorry for the King and Queen who had to mix with them" she confided. It sounded as if the training from Kettering High School had paid off.

Fashion

Annie seems to have been a modern woman, and fashion and politics show this quite visibly. The fashion for long skirts, long sleeves, high collars with supports and frills were the order of the day for long periods of the Victorian age. It is well known that in Victorian society, the sight of a woman's ankles was considered risqué. Clothes were large and encompassing and usually in dull colours. There were very few bright clothes. Annie had a blue skirt and a pink one in linen and at knee length. Fashion changed because of the First World War, when women often took over the jobs formerly done by men. This change in attitude towards women permitted a change in fashion, too. Necks were more open, for example. Women were allowed to have more say in various matters.

Hairstyles underwent a dramatic change too, with hair being cut short and swept severely back. Annie didn't exactly tell me that she adopted this new fashion, but she was certainly sympathetic to it. She talked about 'flappers' in a knowing way. There is much conjecture as to where the term actually came from. In England by the 1890s, the word "flapper" was used in some localities as slang both for a very young prostitute, and, in a more general and less derogatory sense, of any lively mid-teenage girl. The word was also associated with dancing, as the flapper danced like a bird, flapping her arms while doing the Charleston. Another theory is that the term coincided with a fashion among teenage girls in the United States in the early 1920s for wearing unbuckled galoshes, and that they were called "flappers" because they flapped when they walked, as they wore their overshoes or galoshes unfastened, showing that they defied convention in a manner similar to the 21st century fad for untied shoelaces.

Annie's idea was that the term was named after the flapper bracket on a motor bike – a pillion seat. Girls used to sit at the back of the bike and in Annie's words "You sat on it, bumped along and got a pain in your stomach – what you suffered for fashion!" The flapper bracket did not endure, as cars soon supplanted the motorbike. I am sure that the term was named from its use by flappers rather than the other way round. It certainly sounds as if Annie did travel on a pillion seat, however.

Annie always had frizzy hair. When at school for a party she put her hair in curlers as the other girls did, but because her hair was already frizzy it looked quite odd. There were no hairdressers in those days. You could go and have your hair cut and singed with a hot iron. It sealed the ends. Girls with longer hair tied rags in it to help to dry it.

In 1921, just after she was married, she had her hair bobbed, as was the fashion. This was done when she went up to London to stay with a cousin. When she returned

Hats in abundance. When Prince George came to open Peterborough Hospital the crowds were out to greet him, mostly boys and men in caps in this section. Annie commented that it was de rigeur to wear a hat.

home to the Decoy, Billy was absolutely disgusted and didn't speak to her for several days. "He never forgave me" she said.

Votes for Women

Politics come in with the suffragette movement. "People used to tease me and call me a suffragette." She certainly empathised with the women's movement, but did not get involved. "There was very little strength for the movement locally." She did confide in me with a statement that certainly rang true: "I was quite equal to any man."

In 1918, at the very end of the war, the Government passed the Representation of the People Act, giving the vote to all men over 21, as well as all women over the age of 30 who met minimum property qualifications. Thus were 8.4 million women enfranchised. In 1928 the government passed the Representation of the People (Equal Franchise) Act, equalising the franchise to all persons over the age of 21 on equal terms.

Annie was twenty-eight years old at this time, so it would not be too long before she could cast a vote. She remembers talking about the vote to another woman: "This is good news for you as you will be able to vote now." The woman, who was a lot older than Annie, replied "Oh no, I won't be able to vote just yet"; she did not wish to admit her age. Annie said that life did not really change for women – certainly not the ones from the countryside. Local men were largely indifferent to this new act of Parliament.

Social Life

When Annie was a teenager, she used to go to dances quite often. Glinton School was one of the venues. 'Blind Billy' used to play the violin and the piano providing the music for the dances. It was mainly teenagers who attended, though a few older people were present, too. They always finished by midnight. In her later teens she used to go to Forester's Hall in Crowland. She would usually walk, though a lift in a pony and trap was always welcome. "We used to go in big groups. I remember one night when it was really cold and there was thick snow, we put our stockings over our shoes to prevent us slipping over."

There was a lot of card playing, too. Whist drives were very popular. Lots of card games were played at Christmas time, including "silly ones" like 'Donkey'.

In those early days of the twentieth century, most people still went to church. The Williams family travelled by pony and trap to St. Pega's Church in Peakirk. Men and children attended in the morning on a Sunday while mothers went at 3 pm – "because they had to cook the dinners". Gender roles were much more clearly defined in those days, as was social status. Annie further emphasises this in her next statement: "Father used to go into the pub. He paid some chap tuppence to hold his horse for him".

Cinema and Entertainment

The cinema came to Peterborough in about 1910. Annie used to go on a Saturday afternoon to the Palace Picture

House. The cost was 6d and a series of films lasting about five minutes each was shown. The price for children was 2d. "The films were jerky little things."

Most of the early films were comedies, "Custard pies and Charlie Chaplin shorts" as she said. "They must nearly all have been comedies because I cannot remember crying at any of them. There were some westerns and gangster films, but I didn't much care for those. When I did get involved in a dramatic plot, I remember clutching at the person next to me in the audience… even if I didn't know them!"

A good way of ensuring that an audience would return was the serial with its cliff hanger and 'see next week' hook line. "I saw a number of films that had a woman tied up and a railway line with the train coming very fast."

A ground-breaking science fiction play that introduced the word 'Robot' to the world was R.U.R. (*Rossumovi Univerzální Roboti* , Rossum's Universal Robots) in which the robots attempt to take over the world. Annie saw it in a London theatre in the early 1920s. She said it made a lasting impression on her. She had never seen anything like it before.

Some of her very favourite films of the 1930s included 'Beau Geste' with Gary Cooper and 'Gone With The Wind' with Clark Gable, who was another revered actor (posters opposite).

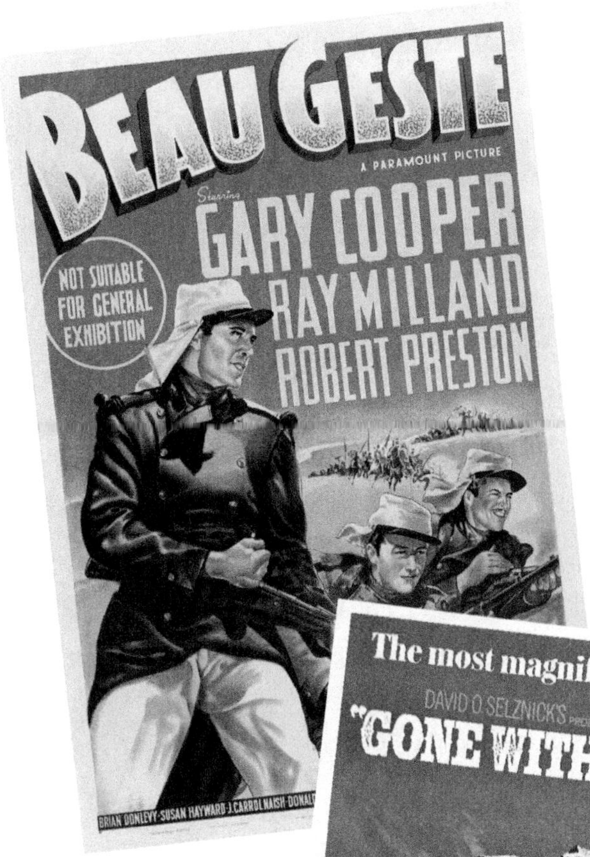
BEAU GESTE
A PARAMOUNT PICTURE
Starring
GARY COOPER
RAY MILLAND
ROBERT PRESTON
NOT SUITABLE FOR GENERAL EXHIBITION
BRIAN DONLEVY · SUSAN HAYWARD · J. CARROL NAISH · DONAL

The most magnificent picture ever!
DAVID O. SELZNICK'S PRODUCTION OF MARGARET MITCHELL'S
"GONE WITH THE WIND"
Winner of Ten Academy Awards
CLARK GABLE
VIVIEN LEIGH
LESLIE HOWARD OLIVIA de HAVILLAND
A SELZNICK INTERNATIONAL PICTURE · VICTOR FLEMING · SIDNEY HOWARD · METRO-GOLDWYN-MAYER INC.
METROCOLOR

"Cinemas at that time were quite big buildings with a stage at the front. There were also tip-up seats which I hadn't seen before."

1907 had seen the building of a very imposing theatre in the form of the Hippodrome. It opened for all the silent films. There was a pianist sitting at the front who helped to bring tension or empathy to what was on the screen. "It was usually a woman who was playing."

When it rained, the disadvantages of having a large tin roof soon became apparent. The theatre was modified to include cinematic film and named the Palladium (9th February 1922) and then went through another name change to the Palace (8th December 1924). Annie remembers visiting each phase of this building for stage shows as well as for the new films at the cinema.

The opening of the Embassy cinema on the site next door in 1937 spelled the end for the theatre, which closed later in the year, in November. The Embassy at its peak drew audiences from an 80-mile radius and was regarded as the sixth best venue in the whole nation.

Annie liked Charlie Chaplin, Buster Keaton and Harold Lloyd. "You could buy Harold Lloyd glasses for a penny at the Peterborough Penny Bazaar. Sometimes a stage show interspersed the films with a juggling act for example.

"Rudolph Valentino, we all fell for him. He died so young. Many women wore black. My all-time favourites were Cicely Courtneidge and her husband Jack Hulbert." Although these two had appeared on the radio, they became more famous during the embryonic talkies era.

"Wait a minute… you ain't heard nothin' yet." These

The Hippodrome, which opened in 1907

were the dramatic spoken words in a scene in 'The Jazz Singer' (1927), which changed the entertainment world and marked the arrival of sound to the movies. Never again would audiences have to read "titles" to explain the action or translate the sweet nothings of lovers. In the space of just over an hour, the silent film was dead.

Annie was part of this revolution in cinema history, as she had travelled to London to see the film. She said she was enthralled by it and that the anticipation had been well worth it. She also commented on the fact that almost overnight many of the famous film actors "who had the wrong sort of voice" were put out of work. This was clearly demonstrated in the classic 'Singing in The Rain' movie by Jean Hagen, whose voice was dubbed by Debbie Reynolds, only for it all to go horribly wrong.

One of the very early 'talkies' had a local connection. It was a filmed version of Galsworthy's play 'Escape' from September 1930. The hunting scenes were filmed at Wansford and featured the Fitzwilliam hounds.

I have mentioned the popularity of ice skating, especially, if not exclusively, when the rivers froze over, but roller

The Peterborough Pavilion Rink, which was close to the Hippodrome and was frequented by Annie.

skating was popular too. Annie tells of hiring skates to use at the rinks near the Cattle Market in Peterborough or one on Broadway.

Annie used to go to London quite frequently Train fare was 3s/9d half-day return. She would leave at midday and return at midnight. "The beauty of this was being able to go shopping and follow it with a meal and a theatre visit." In 1913 she went to see 'Pygmalion' by George Bernard Shaw. She was not necessarily very keen on Shaw but wanted to know what the 'word' was that everyone was talking about and not printed in the newspapers that were not permitted to use swear words. Mrs Patrick Campbell played the part of Eliza Doolittle. "Are you going to walk across the park?" "Not bloody likely!"

In keeping with a lot of Annie's adventures, there was a burst tyre in the latter part of the journey from Peterborough to the Decoy. She got a lift on the step of a bicycle, with her arms around the neck of the rider all the way home.

On another of these London half-day returns she remembered thinking "That's it. No more trains for me". The station was overrun by sailors, many of whom had been drinking, and there was a huge rush for the train, with the result that Annie had to stand up all the way back to Peterborough.

Entertainment on the radio came from a station called 2LO which started (just after Station 2MT) in 1922. "Will made a crystal set from cat's whiskers, a bit of crystal and a little wire. It was maddening trying to catch the station. You could buy a crystal set, but they were expensive. My brother-in-law was talking to a friend and said 'have you got a crystal set? What is it? I'm not sure but I know it has a cup without a handle, a cigar box and various other things including a potato'. If you were lucky you could pick up foreign stations. Expensive sets could cost £1 or more. The cost went up to £2 a valve when they first came out, so it could be £5 or £6 a set. These had a big HMV amplifying horn.

"We had cylinder records in the early part of the century but progressed to 78 machines. Will bought Schubert and Russian ballets – highbrow music. You were supposed to change the needle each time after playing. They were silver and gold. The gold ones lasted a few times. You could buy a pack of 200 for a small sum".

The General Strike, 1926

1926 saw one of the most notable events of the century with the General Strike. Without going into all the details, the owners of the coal mines decided to cut the wages of the miners, which was obviously not a popular move. The Trades Union Congress called the strike to prevent wage reduction and worsening conditions for coal miners. It took place over nine days, from 4 May until 12 May 1926. Key industries came to a standstill, which affected virtually the whole country. In Peterborough, for example, the numerous railwaymen were virtually solid in support of the strike. Even the clerks and supervisors supported the strike, which didn't happen in a number of other places. There were no newspapers for nine days and leaflets were issued to keep people informed.

Annie's family supported the Conservative Government led by Stanley Baldwin. They declared that a nine-month subsidy would be provided to maintain the miners' wages and that a Royal Commission would look into the problems of the mining industry and consider its impact on other industries, families and organisations dependent on coal supplies industry. The army was called upon by the Government as many of the ruling classes became afraid of a revolution.

The *Peterborough Citizen* newspaper reported on 10th May 1926 that there was a lack of enthusiasm among many strikers. Apart from a few younger men, many of those on strike regretted that they had been called out and felt obliged to follow their union's instructions.

Those people who were opposed to the strike took it upon themselves to try to maintain some form of order. A number of young men left their offices to become bus drivers, for example. Annie's brother-in-law, who was a merchant in Covent Garden, experienced some trouble and "equipped his drivers with revolvers and put another man in the cab". Fortunately, nothing happened.

Farm workers were not really affected by the strike. Life on the farms went on as usual, but transporting produce would be a problem. Some farmers drove to London with their tractors, which took an inordinately long time but made their point. Billy had lorries and he also went to London, passing the tractors en route. Annie remembered seeing lorries with potatoes and other produce from Crowland, Spalding and the Deeping area that were headed for London. "In the end people in the country got their backs up and supported the government and Baldwin," said Annie. I am not sure those from the mining communities would agree with her verdict.

The Depression

1929 not only saw the passing of Annie's father but the Wall Street Crash in America, which sent shock waves around the world and heralded what was to become 'the Depression'. A number of the local farmers went bust, the main reason being a shortage of money. Some of the smaller farms and some bigger ones had to sell out. Life at the Decoy remained quite ordinary, however. Like the period during the Great War, the element of self-sufficiency carried the family through.

Annie remembered that food was very cheap. "Biscuits were 3d per pound, I remember," she said. "Bread was awful during the 1930s. We used to get it from a local baker. We asked if the bread was bad because of the depression and he said 'No, I am just an awful baker'. The bread was often not baked in the middle and very doughy. We had a butcher come in and kill the pigs and made sausages. We kept the lard in big soup tureens and it used to last for months. Refrigeration was in the dairy – it was cold in there and we could keep things cool."

There was also a cellar where big barrels of beer were stored. "We used to keep three at a time. The men that were employed at harvest time used to drink a lot of beer. We had a number of workers. There was always a maid, a housekeeper, an under housekeeper, a yard boy, two other boys, three at the Decoy and other casuals at harvest time." She did concede that the newspapers were always a day late because they came by post.

Knowing her views on the General Strike, I asked her about the Jarrow March and, quite typically, she responded, "It held no interest to us. It was a long way off and we just weren't interested". In normal time "we always had the *Daily Mail* and it only cost a halfpenny."

Abdication, 1936

The same year as the Jarrow March saw King Edward VIII's abdication. "We were all shocked. We had heard rumours, but there had been nothing in the newspapers as the press did not cover the story. I was at a tennis party where someone had seen an American paper about the wretched Mrs Simpson. We were glad he abdicated, because we certainly did not want her to be queen. He had been a very popular figure, especially during the First World War and in a number of tours abroad like to India. It was rumoured that he had started drinking and a doctor friend of ours reported that Mrs Simpson was found dead drunk in the gutter and he had to attend to her. I don't think that I believed it as there was a lot of exaggeration in the press at the time. It was perhaps a fairy tale. The government did the right thing.

"We listened to the abdication speech on the radio, all huddled round the set. The King said he couldn't carry on without the woman he loved by his side. We couldn't let him marry her as she had been married twice before. I did feel a

Coronation Celebrations at Peakirk (1937). Three who can be identified are Dave Nunn, Leslie Wilkinson (2nd left front row) and Mr Noble (front row, right)

little sorry for him, but felt he had let the country down. We almost despised him in a way. His younger brother became a good king, but we didn't know much about him. His wife [Queen Elizabeth, The Queen Mother] became very popular."

Chapter 6

ENTER PETER SCOTT

Annie and Billy began their friendship with Peter Scott in 1932 when William Tinsley, a farmer from Holbeach Marsh, introduced him to the Borough Fen Decoy. Scott had just left Trinity College, Cambridge, reading Natural Sciences at first but graduating in the History of Art in 1931. He later studied art in Munich. His mother, Kathleen, had been widowed in 1912 by the death of her husband, the Antarctic explorer Robert Falcon Scott. Some years after Scott's death she married Sir Edward Hilton Young, who was the Conservative Minister for Health (1931-35). She was a noted sculptor.

Kathleen and Edward descended upon the Williams at the Decoy unannounced on a Sunday afternoon, leaving Billy to quickly prepare a teatime meal. Annie recalled that the chauffeur had "egg sarnies in the kitchen" (Kathleen later had a statue erected in the Peakirk home gardens called The Young Viking - see below).

Peter had attended Oundle Public School as a boy and became acquainted with the Headmaster's son, James Fisher, who became a leading ornithologist. It is reputed that Fisher senior said to Kathleen, "Get the boy interested in natural history, it is better than games". Scott was actually a very keen sportsman as well, even representing his country in the 1936 Olympics in Berlin in the sailing and winning a bronze medal.

Peter Scott developed a strong bond with the Williams family and lived with them during the 1931/2 winter. His first impression of the Decoy was strong. "The place and the people were delightful. The decoy technique was fascinating, but I didn't like having to kill the ducks and vowed I would, someday, change that." This did take time to come to fruition and was something that pleased both Billy and Peter, when the time came that the birds did not have to be killed.

This was not until after the Second World War. Having said, that both of them did go shooting but not at the decoy. Holbeach Marshes was the venue for the shooting. There was the story that the two men held the record for the number of geese shot in one session with a punt gun. Their total of seventeen was eventually surpassed by someone claiming nineteen birds.

A punt gun was mounted in a flat boat and had a long barrel. The shooter had to lie down flat and the trigger was activated by pulling a piece of string. The gun was reloaded like an old musket. This was not an easy gun to operate, so the total of kills was certainly an achievement.

The birds at the Decoy were dispatched by Billy in such a neat, clean and instantaneous way that they fetched much higher prices than those that had been shot. Billy locked the wings over their backs causing the birds to lie still without flapping. He would then break their necks close to the skull. A merchant once told him "Your birds look like they had died in their sleep".

Peter Scott with Annie

Peter Scott in Suffolk, feeding the birds

Tony Cook and R.E.M. Pilcher in *The History of Borough Fen* relate an amusing story about the recovery of a Mallard that had been ringed:

"An anxious correspondent wrote a letter to 'The Field' [the world's oldest country and field sports magazine, having been published continuously since 1853] saying he had sent to the British Museum [where all the rings were sent] a ring recovered from a pork pie served to him at a London restaurant. He asked the Museum, since the ring was theirs, to let him know 'what beast had escaped from their care to land on his luncheon plate'. He was told the ring had come from the leg of a mallard, a bird Billy had caught, ringed and released, but which had been shot shortly afterwards.

Annie told me how one February morning Peter got up very early to break the ice. Billy got up a little later, but it was still pitch black. Once outside, Peter asked Billy how he had got to the place where he was and Billy told him; where Peter had broken the ice, Billy had walked over the various fragments of floating ice without slipping into the water. It would have been an invigorating early morning dip.

"When I had known Billy for about three months, I proposed that we build an observation hut and he seemed to be in favour." –

Peter Scott's words from *Eye of the Wind*. This hut was built and was very successful, in that it could be reached in secrecy. Being able to count the birds more accurately was a bonus. It was possible to see how many of each species there were.

Although Scott had done a lot of hunting, he was hoping for the day when the birds could be ringed and not killed.

This was dependent on the economic viability of the Decoy, and it was achieved only a couple of years before Billy's death in 1958. Before then only mallards had been killed, with all other species being ringed and released. This was around 1949.

Peter Scott is also known as a very accomplished painter. During that winter of 1931 he spent a lot of his time sketching the different birds he saw. He would turn these into paintings which within a year or so would be exhibited at Bond Street in London. He also sent three pictures to the Royal Academy and had two of them accepted. Both of them sold. These were painted at the Decoy. One was called 'Pink Feet In A Snow Storm'.

It was at this time, encouraged by Peter Scott, that Annie got very interested in painting. He tended to work outdoors, while she stayed within the confines of the house and painted mainly flowers. Annie still had one of Peter's sketchbooks.

'Black Ducks At Noon' by Peter Scott

Scott's exhibitions in Bond Street became an annual event. At one of these he rushed up to Annie and Billy, who had arrived rather late, saying "Come with me, I want you to meet Sir Samuel Hoare [the Secretary of State for India and later Home Secretary]. These are the two people who have helped me so much."

Annie confided that she did not like the modern diesel trains and bemoaned the passing of the steam age. "They had far more character. It was always reassuring to hear the 'chuff chuff' noise as you were pulling out of the station."

Annie Becomes an Artist

One of the many pleasures in Annie's life was painting. She had started when a very young woman at about twelve or thirteen years of age. It was a subject at school that she had always been keen on. She confessed: "My painting is nothing to talk about. A man at the Peterborough Art School told me, 'your paintings are no good but they are what the man in the street likes'."

She was always able to sell her paintings when those who were considered better could not. I think there was an element of false modesty in Annie's verdict on her work. I saw a number of her paintings, mainly with floral themes, and they were very good.

She started to paint much more seriously when Peter Scott came to stay in the winter of 1932. At school most things she painted were copies. Scott told her, "you don't want to do copies, you must paint from real life." He told her that anyone can draw but not everyone can paint. Annie was never convinced that she could draw, but did concede that she could paint. She used to sit alongside him and he would offer constructive criticism. He always painted outside at the Decoy – his copious bird scenes are now legend – while Annie preferred the comfort of working indoors. His verdict on Annie as a person and a painter is significant. He regarded her as a close friend and "a fine person with a great deal of character. I am very fond of her and think that she has considerable talent as a painter." These words from my 1976 interview with him.

Scott was on a mission. He wanted to paint the wildfowl in a way he saw them. To use his words from *The Eye of the Wind*: "Other artists did not *know* them quite as I knew them. I only had to put on canvas the birds as I had seen them at dawn or dusk or moonlight, or in a storm or frost or snow, and I could not fail to be doing something original. It remained to be seen whether those who looked at the pictures would be moved in the same way that I was when I watched the flight of wild geese, and heard their music."

He worked hard during his time with the Williams and ended up with about forty paintings. He sent three to the Royal Academy for the summer exhibition and managed to get two accepted. Even better, in 1933, of the forty or so that he painted at Borough Fen he sold all bar two or three at a one-man show, making an average of £25 for each one. His stay at the Decoy was described as "very agreeable" and he acknowledged the assistance given to him for the early exhibition work "before moving down to my lighthouse on the Wash."

Annie still had the very first painting she did, on the

back of another later work, in her house - a pewter pot, a pewter plate and a bowl of flowers. She used oils for all her work. She was often short of wood or canvas, so she tended to paint on both sides. That same year, 1932, she sold a painting at the Peterborough Art Exhibition - "It was the only one that sold". She made £1 from it, which backed up the earlier words of the Art Society critic.

Meetings were held above the old Butter Market which was in the Market Square Town Hall in what is called Cathedral Square. "We had to climb the stairs into the room above. When the new Town Hall was built in Bridge Street in 1933, we had to move."

We met at Mrs Kant's house in Walton. Her husband (Commander Kant) was one of the directors at Peter Brotherhood. "They had a very big house." Things were set out for the members to paint, still life objects. Exhibitions were held annually in the Butter Market and, from there, in the new Town Hall and finally at Brook Street (which became the Adult Education Centre).

"Later on, I used to sell my paintings at Peakirk when I used to do the teas at the Wildfowl Trust. People would come in and say 'I like that' and buy it. A man once bought three of my paintings." Annie's favourite painters were Sir Peter Scott (not surprisingly) and Paul Nicholas, a disabled man and a renowned artist. Both of these men were noted for the representation of birds and birdlife. She left the Art Society in 1971 and was still painting at that time at over eighty years of age.

Beer and Pubs

She recalled that when the Wildfowl Trust opened, a pub called the Black Bull changed its name to the Ruddy Duck. This apparently caused some consternation, as some people regarded it as swearing. She mentioned other pubs from years ago – the Boat and the Railway, the latter being converted into a general shop. When she was a little girl there was only one shop, which was a general store. "You could buy tea loose from big canisters and they would weigh it out for you. We used to buy a pound of tea. We used to buy coffee, too, and it was ground at the Decoy. It was a lot of trouble to grind, but my granddad liked it for breakfast." The Peakirk pubs at that time were ale houses and would feature local brews. They did not sell spirits.

Beer was always made at the Decoy in two huge coppers with one inside. The beer was of less quality in the second of the two barrels and was available to the workmen who could go to the outside one, Small Beer Place, and help themselves. "This was long before my time, but the place retained its name," she said. The barrels were so big that when empty, you could stand inside one without being seen. Home-made wines were very popular; rhubarb, redcurrant, elderberry and gooseberry, which was claimed to be as good as sherry.

Services in the area were very different then, too. The postal service operated without real Post Offices. The postmen were not regular people and had no uniform as such – "Ours used to be the baker boy." You could collect your mail, too, from the general store. It was here that you could

Annie at Decoy Farmhouse, feeding the ducks

purchase stamps in small books. It was 1d for regular mail and 1/2d for unsealed letters and postcards.

These were very popular. "I used to collect the ones with famous actresses on. Zena Dare was my big favourite. We would then put them in albums." Zena Dare was photographed with skates at Olympia, at a time when roller skating was all the rage – one of Annie's passions. Perhaps this influenced the favouritism.

Zena Dare, Annie's favourite actress

Chapter 7

INTO THE SECOND WORLD WAR

<hr>

Peter Scott was a frequent visitor to the Decoy and even though his mother was at home in London (not that far down the Great North Road), he preferred to spend Christmas 1931 with the Williams. He was at the Williams house when the news broke that Adolf Hitler had triumphed in the 1933 elections in Germany. Quite accurately he predicted "Oh dear, that will be the end! That means war." Annie said they expected war at any time after that and had no time for "Hitler's silly speeches and shouting about".

Later, when Neville Chamberlain, the Conservative Prime Minister, returned from Munich waving his piece of paper (the agreement with Hitler), Annie thought "peace in our time? That's going to do no good. It only delayed the war for one year. Most people roared with laughter. The general public were not fooled".

The Williams household were very staunch Winston Churchill fans. They heeded his prophetic speeches in the lead up to the war and were not surprised when he took over from Chamberlain. Annie then, very impressively, recited the "Fight on the beaches" speech like someone who had learned a poem when young and had never forgotten it:

"We shall go on to the end. We shall fight in France, we shall fight on the seas and oceans, we shall fight with growing confidence and growing strength in the air, we shall defend our island, whatever the cost may be. We shall fight on the beaches, we shall fight on the landing grounds, we shall fight in the fields and in the streets, we shall fight in the hills; we shall never surrender."

She finished with a triumphant smile. Probably wisely, did not attempt a Churchill impersonation.

War broke out on 3rd September 1939. "It was a Sunday. We heard Chamberlain on the radio informing us 'We are at war with Germany'. They hadn't replied to our demands. It was awful. We all expected that bombs would be dropping all over the place. You always felt that a German plane was coming specially to drop a bomb on you."

Annie was in Peterborough when the air raid siren went off on one occasion. "I was walking with a friend, and she had little imagination. No bombs were ever going to drop on her. All the shops shut. People were madly rushing to and fro. Soon everywhere was deserted. It was a false alarm. Nothing happened."

In 1940 Winston Churchill broadcast for men to form

the Home Guard. They were needed now that there was a real risk of invasion. Most men who could fight were already in the forces, and those that were left were either too young, too old, or in reserved occupations (those jobs vital to the war effort). The government was expecting 150,000 men to volunteer for the Home Guard. Within the first month, 750,000 men had volunteered, and by the end of June 1940, the total number of volunteers was over one million. The number of men in the Home Guard did not fall below one million until they were stood down in December 1944.

There were two Home Guard units in the Peterborough area, the Northamptonshire Home Guard Battalion and the Soke of Peterborough Battalion, covering the area from Dogsthorpe, out through Newborough to Eye and beyond, a vulnerable area of some eighty square miles.

The BBC's enduring sitcom "Dad's Army" presented a different impression of the Home Guard. It is true they drilled with sticks and First World War weapons, but they were generally earnest people who could not contemplate Hitler taking over this nation

The Government issued instructions about gas masks. After the horrors of the First World War, it was anticipated that there would be gas attacks on civilians. "The masks were like snouts. We had to go to the local school to learn about them, how to fit them et cetera. You had to go everywhere with them, carrying them in a cardboard box fastened with string."

The local doctor came to the village school. "We were

given lessons in first aid. It was a soft business really. There was an exam, but we hadn't been at it long enough. We hardly knew anything. We were tested for slings, broken arms and legs, splints et cetera. We really didn't know the first thing about it. There was a chap from Newborough who had been through it before and he played the part of the patient. He stood behind the doctor and mouthed the answers to us when the doctor asked his questions. Then we were supposed to bandage broken legs. The patient got on the stretcher himself and tied the bandages up. We just did the knots at the end. We all passed!

"Churchill did keep the country together during the war. He made very good speeches. At Dunkirk (where 300,000 troops were returned from France by hundreds of civilian helpers), we couldn't believe that all those little boats and ships came to the rescue. We knew then that we were not going to lose. We did expect, like the first war, that it would go on for a long time. Germany couldn't beat the USA and would not be able to hold out for ever." There may be a touch of hindsight in this verdict, but it was certainly typical of the British people. Churchill's speech did ring true.

The Williams house had evacuees right from the start of the war. In the first three days of official evacuation, 1.5 million people were moved: 827,000 children of school age, 524,000 mothers and young children (under 5), 13,000 pregnant women, 70,000 disabled people and over 103,000 teachers and other 'helpers'. Children were parted from their parents and sent to many places in the country where, it was hoped, there would be little if any sign of warfare. By the end of the war around 3.5 million people, mainly children, had experienced evacuation.

A schoolmaster named Bell, from London, came down and stayed in the capital during the blitz. He stayed for a few years afterwards as well. He taught the (mainly evacuee) children at the nearby Newborough Village Hall. He paid about thirty shillings a week for his food and keep. Host families could expect to receive payment via the post office (ten shillings and sixpence, worth about £28 in today's money, for the first unaccompanied child and eight shillings and sixpence for any subsequent children).

There were also Land Army girls in this rural area and one was supposed to stay with the Williams. "She was a girl from a cigarette factory in the East End of London. She was useless. We said to her that she wouldn't like it there. It's ever so lonely. She ran away and we never saw her again. She got into trouble for it, but never came back with us.

"The Government tried to get us to grow more crops. War Agriculture Committees were set up. They were a perfect nuisance. They didn't know any more than anyone else. We ignored them. 'Dig For Victory' was for townspeople. They came and collected all the railings to make armaments from the metal. They never used them and they were still in a scrapyard for many years after the war. Our crops were sold to corn and potato merchants, the same as in peace time, who in turn sold them to the Ministry".

Observer Corps

Billy was fifty-seven years old when war was declared in 1939. He served in the Observer Corps, which was described by Jon Lake, an author and contributor to aviation magazines, as "arguably the most valuable of the voluntary services". Annie recalled "He had to wear a beret". The observers on the ground were tasked with estimating the height at which the German Luftwaffe formations flew and their bearing. Numbers and types of aircraft would have to be relayed back to their Group Headquarters. This information was then fed to the RAF, who determined what course of action to take. His other duties were to report any crashes, where the plane had landed and if the pilot had managed to parachute. There were Observer Corps groups every few miles, covering the country. The local station was quite close. The men took it in turns to keep watch for four hours (midday till four o' clock, four o' clock till eight and so on).

Annie, who was left at the Decoy, was not worried. She did see a German plane shot down and the pilot parachuted out. The plane came down in Northborough and she watched it being chased by British planes and saw all the tracer bullets. The pilot was arrested. "I did have my three dogs for company."

On the night of the Coventry raid (14th November 1940) "it seemed as though the whole of the German air force was in the skies. German planes made a different noise. You could always tell them from the British. We got underneath the dining table, which was very heavy, and stayed there most of the night." The raid on Coventry was a major one and resulted in over 450 people being killed and 700 seriously wounded. Some 230 German planes took part in this raid, in which, infamously, the Cathedral was destroyed.

However, in all honesty, being stuck out at the Decoy,

Billy did not have that much to report. There was the night when a large landmine fell close to Newborough. Billy had heard the whining noise, followed by a muffled explosion. It left a huge crater in a ploughed field next to the Peterborough to Crowland road.

On the A47 by the side of the Newborough Road, a large area was dug in which to place the dead when Peterborough was bombed. Fortunately, it was never required. Peterborough, with its heavy industry factories like Peter Brotherhoods, had expected to be a target, but was only seriously attacked once. Annie told me that many people in the city set fires going to make it look from the air as if the German raid was a great success.

My favourite Brotherhoods story is of the guy with a machine gun stationed high up next to the main north-south railway line where the factory was. His task was to fire on any German aircraft that were making their way back home after a raid and following the railway lines as a good navigational aid. Only once during the whole of the war, towards the end, did a German plane fly along this route and the gunner was so shocked that he could not get the cover off the gun in time.

Many Allied planes were unloaded so that they could fly more quickly when returning home. Billy often saw planes going past. There was one from RAF Wittering (near Stamford) flying overhead with its bomb doors wide open. It was not very high and he could clearly see the men inside.

Of all the sightings during the war, the most memorable one that Billy experienced was that of the Hollywood actor Clark Gable, star of the major film success 'Gone With

The Wind' (1939). He was going past in a jeep in Long Causeway, Peterborough. Gable was stationed at RAF Polebrook with the 351st Bomb Group in 1943. (He flew five combat missions, including one to Germany, as an observer-gunner in B-17 Flying Fortresses between May 4 and September 23, 1943, earning the Air Medal and the Distinguished Flying Cross for his efforts).

Billy commented that the First World War "spoiled my young life absolutely". He did contract malaria while in Mesopotamia and was hospitalised several times. He suffered with occasional bouts of it again during the rest of his life: "Wars are a great waste." Though he was not in action as such during the Second World War, this feeling never really left him.

Rationing

Billy always kept on very friendly terms with the police. "He was allowed to have whatever guns he needed," Annie recalled. "He always kept a revolver during the war and slept with it, loaded, by the bedside. A warden came to the Decoy once shouting that some Germans were loose in the area. Billy went out with his revolver looking behind all the trees. Of course, he found nothing, but it did seem scary at the time."

After petrol, January 1940 saw bacon, butter and sugar being rationed. Meat, tea, jam, biscuits, breakfast cereals, cheese, eggs, lard, milk, canned and dried fruit were rationed subsequently, but not all at once. Fruit and vegetables were very limited in numbers. The 'Dig For Victory' programme was designed to produce much more.

Annie remembered that toothpaste came wrapped in cardboard and the newspapers were made of much coarser paper and had fewer pages. The daily papers were 1d and it was 2d for a Sunday newspaper.

Billy's friendship with the local constabulary stood him in good stead when his car, a Ford 8, was stopped and checked with regard to the petrol allowance. Petrol had been the very first item to be rationed because all petrol at that time came from overseas. In 1942 petrol for private use was withdrawn and only available for essential work. You had to have a permit to prove this.

All large cars were taken by the state and converted into vans and ambulances; the nation had to come first. As a result of the hard rationing of petrol many people decided not to drive anyway. With the blackout rules it was dangerous to be on the roads. (See 'Black Out Mishap' where this proved to be a major problem for Billy and Annie).

You were not supposed to leave your own area either. Rationing was introduced as in the Great War, but the inhabitants of the Decoy were still able to survive through their self-sufficiency as they had before.

It was the clothing coupons that caused most anxiety with Annie. She used many coupons to get the muslin for making butter and had none left for buying any clothes. "It really didn't matter in the end because no one went out with smart clothes. It was wartime."

Billy was stopped en route to Borough Fen when he was on his way to join a regular shooting syndicate. This was not a designated special circumstance, and he was lucky to

A typical shop window notice during the war. Billy's family business included potatoes and was untroubled by this.

get off with a warning. There were fines for breaking this law. Billy's smooth talking did the trick.

The Williams played tennis and bridge a lot during the war. There was a court at the Decoy, "but we were not very good." Many farmers had tennis courts and tennis parties were quite common, especially in the summer months. Annie confided that when they were going out socially, they would pile loads of farm produce in the back of the car in case they were stopped. They could then claim to be on farming business. There was a petrol allowance for farm machinery, which they obviously took advantage of.

Annie remembers putting the brown paper in the Decoy windows for blackout. The paper was stuck to a wooden structure which was then hung up. "Nobody ever came to check on us. We were too far out. There was none of that 'Put that Light Out' from the wardens in bigger cities and towns."

Wartime Radio

During the Second World War, the radio came into its own. With restrictions on entertainment, you could listen to the good old wireless sitting in the comfort of your home. The iconic radio show of the war was ITMA (It's That Man Again), starring Tommy Handley. It ran from 1939 beyond the end of the war until 1949. Both Annie and Billy liked the programme, with Arthur Askey being a particular favourite. The show featured comic situations that were mostly related to current war news. It featured popular characters like Colonel Chinstrap and Mrs Mopp, whose "Can I do you now, sir?" catchphrase was echoed around the country. In terms of light relief from the war, this show provided just the tonic for morale during the dark days.

Someone else that the Williams listened to during the war and regarded as a comic was Lord Haw Haw. This was the name given to US-born British Nazi sympathiser William Joyce, who made regular German propaganda programmes that were full of inaccuracies and exaggerations. His affected way of speaking gave him his nickname. Annie's "Gairmany calling" impression showed how well remembered this programme was and how serious its impact was. Many families listened in the hope of finding what had happened to family members, but of course Joyce was never going to intentionally give any information away. "We regarded him as a big joke and used to think the opposite of what he said would be true." He was found guilty of treason and executed at Wandsworth prison on 3 January 1946. It is estimated that he had six million regular listeners in Britain and occasionally as many as eighteen million.

On a much lighter note, Gert and Daisy were a comedy duo who talked about a host of trivial things and another act liked by Annie in particular. They were the sisters of Jack Warner, who became the nation's favourite policeman as Dixon Of Dock Green on TV. They were on the show 'Workers Playtime' which started in 1941 and was broadcast from factory canteens, dockyards and other places of work throughout the country. It was a highly popular and successful entertainment show initially designed to lift public morale. It was on three times a week and ran till 1964.

Taking the radio programmes to a personal level, Billy was actually in a couple of shows well after the war. In the first he was with a group of about half a dozen different characters talking about things from the British way of life. Somebody would talk about bee keeping, for instance. Billy talked about the Decoy. He later appeared on a show that in its heyday attracted over 20 million listeners – 'Have A Go'. It was hosted by Wilfred Pickles and his wife, Mabel, and toured the nation with broadcasts from church halls, factory canteens and the like. This one, from neighbouring Crowland, featured Billy talking about his life at the Decoy again. Annie used to accompany him when he was on a broadcast, but always stayed in the background.

Wartime Entertainment

During the blitz a lot of the theatre productions were moved to the provinces. Annie and Billy went to see the musical "Lilac Time" at the Embassy Theatre in Peterborough with Ivor Novello. It cost them 7/6d. Going to the pictures in 1940 would have cost only 10d by comparison.

Quite naturally from a practical point of view, entertainment was cut back during the war. Petrol rationing, costs, the darkness as well as the risk of being bombed played their part. Pubs did not shut but Annie recalled how they were "not nice places to go in". Because the doors and windows had to be kept shut, she remembered nearly choking on the smoky atmosphere." Whenever we went into Peterborough, we used to try to park at The Bull Hotel car park in Westgate".

Blackout Mishap

The black-out meant that there no street lights, so on a moonless or cloudy night, it was virtually pitch black everywhere. "We had been to the pictures and when we came out it was blacker than ever. We hadn't realised just how dark it was going to be. We hadn't got a torch and couldn't find the car for ages. You could use your sidelights when driving but they were not really that good. Perhaps we should have learned our lesson for later that year we were invited to a Christmas party. We were going along the Decoy drive, which had a deep dyke one side and wagon tracks the other. The Muscovy ducks always used to park themselves on the wagon side. This time they had moved to the other side – the dyke side. This threw all the navigation awry with the car expecting the road to be where it always was with the ducks to the right.

We slowly toppled over and rolled into the dyke, which was quite deep, but with only a little water at the bottom and plenty of mud. The car was upside down. My husband, who was slimmer than me, managed to open one of the doors and slide out. I couldn't get my door open as it was pressed against the dyke side. I eventually extricated myself but at the cost of going up to my knees in mud and water. I had a short skirt on and got cold, black mud right up my legs. We had to go back into the house to change. My stockings were ruined. I could not find the house key. It had been lost in the inverted car. We both wanted to go to the party and, luckily, I knew a way into the house. I was able to wiggle the kitchen window a few times until it was forced open. We climbed in, got changed and washed and rang up the hosts to explain the situation as to why we would be late.

We got our bikes out and cycled all the way there. When men came the next morning to pull the car out, they drove past it as they couldn't see it. There was a note on the vehicle which we had put on to say that the owners were all right and had not drowned – but even this had not been seen. They eventually fetched a tractor and pulled it right out.

"Our local pub was the Red Cow at Milking Nook near Newborough. It later changed its name to The Decoy."

The Red Cow

There is an apocryphal story to by the landlord, Ted Browning, that they changed the name of the pub because Mrs Browning was tired of people asking if she was the Red Cow when she answered the phone.

Aftermath of the War

"We had heard some of the stories about how the Jews had been treated. We remembered the First War when many exaggerated stories were made against the Germans, so we did not believe that the bodies of dead Jews were being used for making soap and grease. Or of the mass extermination of the race. The real news, the truth, when it was finally exposed horrified us beyond belief. I had thought that when Hess flew to England that this was a sign of weakness and felt that the Germans could not hold out for ever. We never doubted Winston's resolve. The role of the USA made all the difference. We held parties all week among friends. There was one at the Decoy to celebrate the end of the war. We listened to it on the wireless."

Chapter 8

THE ESTATE SOLD OFF

In 1919, after the Great War, all 300,000 acres of the Borough Fen estate was sold off. The buyer was James Watson, an industrialist, under the brand name 'OCO' (Olympia Oil & Cake Co) produced animal feeds for dairy cows, calves, lambs and pigs from a new source – linseed oil. He invested heavily into agricultural estates which included Borough Fen. The farmers from the estate were turned out and were given six months to go. The Williams' house and Decoy – all 200 acres – were kept, however, albeit for only one year.

A Mrs Hanbury had been the owner of the Decoy for most of Mrs Williams' life. When she died her nephew, Colonel Freemantle, put it in the hands of Knight, Frank & Rutley, who sold it. No one was informed what was going on. Most of the local farmers could have bought their own land if they had been given the chance, but they had been told that the whole estate had been sold. This was a major scandal. The ill feeling at the time was unable to manifest itself in any positive way.

All of the horses were sold including those from the Decoy, along with ploughs, harrows, rollers, threshing machines, wagons and carts. The bullocks, pigs, calves and eight cows in a barn were all sold at auction at the Decoy farm. Annie said that she wasn't really aware of this side of things and didn't really miss it apart from maybe the horses, which she loved.

To summarise this complex situation, the Decoy, the farmhouse and much surrounding land, which had never actually been owned by any member of the Williams family, changed hands. Billy was given the lease of the Decoy and house that he and Annie lived in.

The Decoy Farmhouse

Billy Williams repairing one of the pipes at Borough Fen Decoy

Arthur Hill

Arthur Hill was a yardman, a decoy man and an assistant to the Williams family who had first started work for Annie's grandfather. He also looked after the cattle and helped with the catching of the ducks. He could not read or write, which was not untypical, especially in rural areas. He always signed his name with a cross. He wore old clothes with his trousers tied just below the knee, often corduroy, and wore leather boots that got hard after getting wet. These were expensive, and Annie said he should have rubbed goose fat into them. Studded clogs were worn, too.

"A man called John Boyden came from Market Deeping, measured you and made your own personal boots. Everyone wore boots all the time – ones that buttoned up one side. We called them clod hoppers. They cost about 7/6d.

They lasted very well even though we had them soled and heeled quite often.

"Wellies came in later, but not till wartime. When wellies came in, we never wore anything else around the Decoy. We didn't even have mackintoshes. There were lots of times when we wanted to go out but couldn't because we had no proper rainwear. Some people had capes that were supposed to be waterproof but weren't. Some of the labourers wore moleskin hats which they had made themselves – like Davy Crockett hats. These men did work through the rain. They tied sacks around themselves, but that gave very little protection."

Arthur Hill worked for the Williams family for about fifty years and despite his lack of education regarded himself as an expert at the Decoy. He used to annoy the normally gregarious Billy by blaming him for all sorts of things. Cook and Pilcher cite the story that just after Hill's retirement, Billy would never be told again when the ducks they had hoped to take flew out of a pipe. "They 'eard you – it was always 'you', for no duck had ever been known to have heard Hill - or when he acted, often on Hill's advice, that 'that was no way to set about the job'."

Tony Cook started work at the Decoy in 1956 and took over from full time when Billy died in 1958. All the birds caught there were now being ringed. Bird migration could be more easily monitored. One duck that Billy ringed was found in Mongolia and a teal was identified in Newfoundland. The man who found the teal actually went to Peakirk and visited the Wildfowl Trust all the way from Canada.

Crowland

Annie was slightly disparaging about Crowland, as it was in the early 20th Century. "It was five miles from anywhere, and five miles was a long way to walk!" Most of the population had never been outside it. This was not untypical of many fenland villages and towns. "We had a maid from there once who had never even seen the railway. We sent her into Peakirk once and she saw her first train. The people from Crowland were very insular. It was a very isolated place."

The old and the unemployed used to congregate around Trinity Bridge, a unique three-way stone arch bridge that stands at the heart of the town. It used to span the River Welland and a tributary, but that has all been re-routed. It has three stairways that meet at the top and people used to sit on the steps and even the seats under the bridge. "If farmers needed people to work, this would be the first place to look. It was a sort of unofficial labour exchange." This same thing happened at the Guildhall in Peterborough.

There was no welfare state then and those who were unemployed and had no money or food would end up in the workhouse. In Peterborough this was at St. Johns, Thorpe Road. Jobs done were washing, bottle washing, scrubbing floors etc. Crowland had a Doss House which was at the top of West Street at 'The Ship'. "You had to pay 1d or so for a night. There used to be a lot of beggars around. I remember sitting, with a boyfriend, on the bank and giving a tramp a shilling to go to the Doss House at the Ship."

Billy Williams repairing one of the pipes at Borough Fen Decoy

Crowland was basically a small agricultural town. Close to Trinity Bridge was George Williams (no relation), the ironmongers. The other two main general shops were Fillinghams and Willfords. The main entertainment was held at the Forester's Hall, where they used to have concerts.

Annie used to cycle to Crowland for piano lessons from the age of seven. "It was not because I was musical. I was no good at all. It was the accepted thing. One learned the piano or the violin. For me it was a way of getting out and about. Most people had a piano in those days. Everyone gathered round it for a singsong. We made our own entertainment then – 'Daisy, Daisy' was a popular song and 'The Soldiers of the Queen'. A lot of the songs came from the Music Hall in Peterborough. We didn't go, although I went to an Operatic Society's version of the Gilbert and Sullivan classic 'The Pirates of Penzance'. It was very good."

The 1947 Floods

The exceptional weather of 1947 had some horrific effects. In the January of that year it snowed heavily for days,

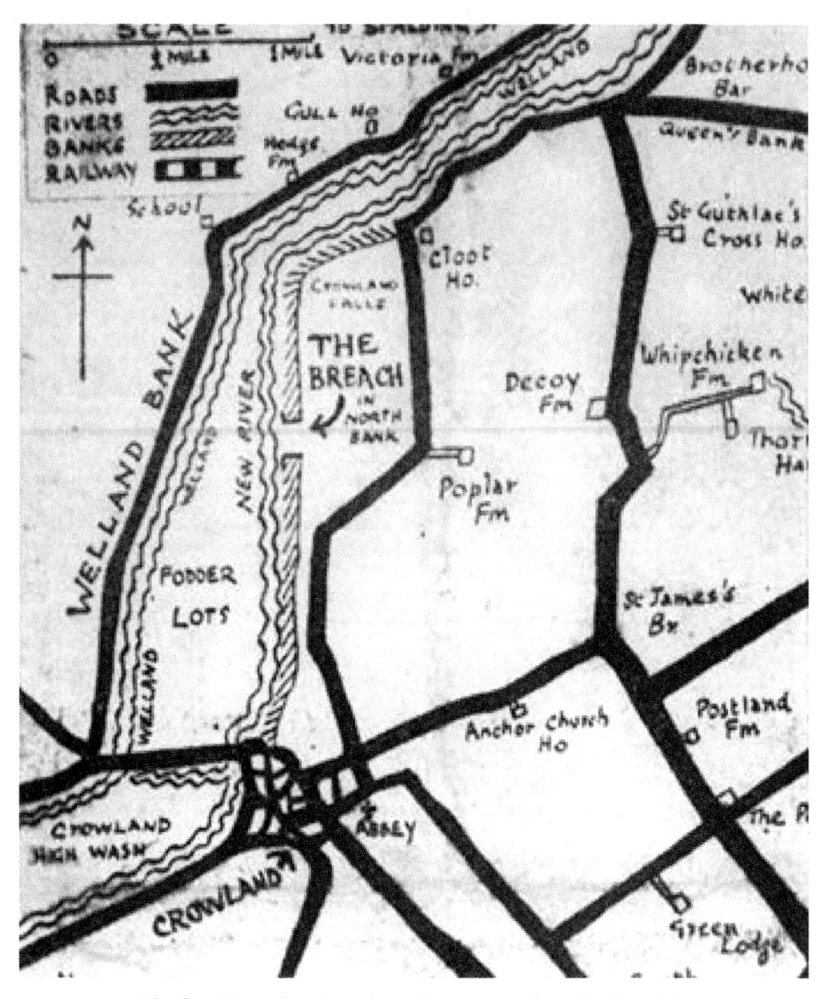

The flood site, showing where the river was breached in 1947

leaving massive drifts of snow whipped up by biting winds. "There was a terrific drift at the Decoy, between the garage and the house. Will cut a doorway through the snow for us to get out. I remember one night when I was walking to Crowland along the bank, the snow was three feet deep. I had to stay in a tied cottage that night as I could not get back. We all caught the flu – Will's parents, his sister and husband, who were living with us at that time."

In early March there were further extremely strong gales and the really heavy snowstorms that followed led to blizzard conditions. The snow drifted up to 15 feet in some parts. When the bitingly cold weather (temperatures were recorded as low as -21 C (-6 F) ended, the temperature rose rapidly. There was still frozen ground and the snow that was thawing at a fast rate had nowhere to go but into the local streams and rivers. The River Welland breached its banks until Crowland was virtually surrounded.

Everyone was expected to help in this national catastrophe. People filled bags with clay and parked them on top of banks five high but the water still burst through. Annie and a woman from the now derelict First Toll Bar used to stay up all night making sandwiches and cups of tea for the men working along the bank. She remembered that she went to look at the floods in the chase and noticed that the water level at the neighbouring farm had dropped about six inches.

Billy went with Annie to see the burst banks at Crowland (see photo below). "A huge slice of bank was missing and the water was pouring like a giant waterfall through the gap. It covered Thorney Fen and Borough Fen and almost reached the Decoy". This was only partly flooded. Billy and Annie's car had broken down and a man who was working at Dowmac and staying with the Williams had gone home, taking his car with him, so the Williams were stranded and helpless. While they were working out what to do, a car approached and they flagged it down. It was Peter Scott. "We rushed out to greet him and I threw my arms around him. We were saved. We had a car to get back home. Peter stayed for the weekend."

This was a time for reflection. Had anyone predicted that it would flood like this? Annie recalled that she had cycled along the bank when the men were putting the clay sacks in place and you could already see the water seeping through because "they were porous". She noted that if the banks had burst right there then the Decoy would be in deep trouble. Instead the following morning it had burst at Crowland.

A young man named Whitsed, the son of farmer Samuel Molson Whitsed, from Little Postland, took command and organised the remedial work. It was thought that the water would ruin the farmland. However, it served to 'make' some people. The soil was not ruined but rather conversely strengthened by the large amount of silt that was brought from neighbouring Lincolnshire and Leicestershire.

Many young lads from Peterborough went around in boats rescuing people, poultry and animals. "Will and I travelled down the Thorney Road, which had not been flooded, and saw a long row of horses being driven away. I also remember seeing an old woman who came out of her cottage after the banks had burst proclaiming 'Something will have to be done, you know, we can't have this.' She was almost Canute-like in her optimism that the water would recede quickly. She did not want to believe it, but she had to when she was rescued. The water had eventually come up to her bedroom window."

Annie walked around the Decoy. "The water came up to the top of my wellingtons. It was a long time before it went away – there was no harvest that year and there were no ducks caught at the decoy either. The Postland farmers were well compensated, even ordinary householders". Compensation was paid out quite quickly. Sluice gates were built to prevent future flooding and arrangements made for the future evacuation of people.

The Return of Winston Churchill

At the end of the Second World War, Winston Churchill was voted out by a huge Labour landslide. Billy and Annie were upset by this and were further disappointed when Peter Scott narrowly failed to be elected to the House of Commons as the member for Wembley North in the same election. He had stood as a Conservative. Annie could see that Britain was losing its world power status and didn't like it. "We 'owned' a large part of the world, but kept giving it away. Queen Victoria was Empress of India, but that was given away, too. We kept winning wars but losing land. The character of England changed. Too much money ruins life. People were happier and life was much simpler before the war. Things were more proper, then."

Things did look up for the Williams when Churchill was voted back into power in 1951. "He had warned about Russia and the Iron Curtain. He was the man for us".

Speaking about the soon-to-become Queen Elizabeth II, Annie described Princess 'Lizzie' as a 'pretty little thing'. There was no speculation about who she would marry, as there was with Princess Margaret according to Annie. "We watched the Coronation at home in 1953. It was a rainy old day but a magnificent ceremony. My friend Peter Scott did some of the commentary on TV. I was actually introduced to the Queen herself when she opened the new building at Slimbridge in 1963."

WWT Slimbridge, is a wetland wildlife reserve in Gloucestershire, set up by Peter Scott and opened in November 1946.

An Unwelcome Move

There was never electricity at the Decoy. It was always oil and paraffin lamps with candles employed at times. "Reading in bed by candlelight was not very good." The Williams left the Decoy in 1949 and moved into a small house in Peakirk. "I hated it. Will wouldn't sell anything, which meant we were overcrowded. The problem at the Decoy had been that as tenants, we were never in control of anything. We were turned out of the Decoy when the Harris family ("self-made people" Annie dubbed them) bought it. One of the sons was going to get married and his future wife took a liking to the house, so it was bought for her. The farm was also owned by the Harris family. The Williams family were for so long occupants at the farmhouse but, crucially as it would turn out, never the owners.

Two very prestigious people came down and supported the Williams family case. Earl Fitzwilliam and Miriam Rothschild tried to get the best Kings Counsel in London to fight the eviction order, but they were just too late. A few months later a law was passed stating that people could not just be turned out of their holding. "There was so much ill-feeling. We moved into the smaller house. It had five bedrooms, which sounded good, but they were all very small rooms. A letter from Herbert Morrison (and Labour MP) Lord President of the Council arrived stating that the eviction had to be delayed, but to no avail. Nothing could be done.

"It was a shock. It was terrible to be turned out after centuries at the Decoy. The family first started there in the year 1670."

It must have been traumatic having to eventually leave the place where your family had lived for all that time, but the reality was that they had never actually owned it. "The KCs for the two parties eventually settled out of court. They took the house and the farm and we kept the Decoy". There had been some talk of Peter Scott buying it, but it all came to nothing.

After the turmoil from the 1919 Borough Fen sale, the house at the Decoy was bought by Billy's brother and a Covent Garden merchant called Jackson. They owned it from 1919 up to 1940. Mr Harris paid £8,259 for it.

The Decoy farmhouse was part-owned by Ernest Jackson and Billy's brother from 1919 till 1940.

The Williams were at this small house in Glinton Road for six years. Billy continued to work at the Decoy. "In 1955 the present Peakirk house appeared on the market and Will said, 'You'd better buy that so I did.'" When asked about how much she was prepared to pay by the Building Society, Annie's instructions were very precise and clear.

"Buy it? Money no object! I was prepared to pay anything." The final sale price was £2,250 for the house and land and there were quite a number of acres.

This old stone-built thatched cottage was built in 1730 and came with five acres of land "As soon as we moved into the new house, we started work on it straight away. We excavated out the back and made a pond." This was to be where the flamingos were "stationed" later. A great deal of work was done by the Wildfowl Trust in 1956 prior to opening the following year. This was a much happier move for Annie.

One of the Peakirk Local Councillors managed to rescue this plaque a number of years ago from the Wildfowl Trust. It is a great artefact and lasting memory of the Waterfowl Gardens. Annie was certainly a witness to this being 'planted' at the official opening. (Photograph courtesy of the Peakirk Parish Council).

The land was a wilderness. "I thought it would be good for a smaller version of Slimbridge. We made representation to Peter Scott, who once he had seen it, agreed." This plot of land formed the basis for the Waterfowl Gardens of the Wildfowl Trust. Billy was created the first curator of the Gardens. Both he and Annie were overjoyed. Billy had been in ill health in the early fifties, almost losing his sight at one point, and this was an affirmation that things were looking up. In 1956 he was joined by Tony Cook, who later on assumed the duties of the routine work at the Decoy.

The Goshams, the Peakirk house from 1955 onwards, and below the back garden with the pond which Annie helped to create.

A Treasure Trove

Annie's house was a treasure trove for antiques. Many were handed down from the Decoy but others were bought by her and Billy. "My husband bought a lot of guns. He had blunderbusses, duelling pistols and others. He went to auctions all over the local area. Most of these items were housed at the Decoy and we didn't bring much after moving to Peakirk."

She described an interesting little gun that was no bigger than 1½ inches. "It's in full working order and made by an ancestor who was an ironmonger from Spalding. He died in 1825. My own personal favourite is an old blue jug. No one has been able to put a date to it, but it is most certainly pre-Victorian. It looks almost like glass but isn't. There is a grandfather clock from the 1700s that has been handed down. It tells the moon's phases and the days of the month. You could tell it was old because the maker, a man named Wilson, had the 's' in his name written like a fancy 'f'."

Research tells us that it was probably the work of James Wilson, who is listed in *Watch and Antique Clock Makers of the World, Volume 2* as working in Stamford between 1786-99. This grandfather clock was housed in the kitchen at the Decoy.

There was also a painting of Annie's great-great-grandfather John Williams, who died in 1825 aged 85. "People have said that in the portrait he looks about sixty years old, which would date the picture to about 1800." There is no signature, so we do not know who painted it. It is thought that master portrait painters used to travel around the country and paint the face but then leave the rest of the work to their students. The hands look completely different in style to the rest of the painting. The face is very good.

There is also a miniature of Ann, the wife of Joseph Williams (1793 -1871). "She was a very fat woman of 22 stones – she died in 1863." In *The History of Borough Fen* (Cook and Pilcher) there is an amusing story about this woman, which emphasises the stereotypical gender roles of Victorian England. I reproduce it here:

"In, presumably her slimmer days, she was accustomed to ride to market side-saddle on the horse behind her husband. Once when he returned home, he called to his wife to dismount. When there was no reply he turned round and found no Ann. In great distress he rode back and several miles away he found a bruised but still smiling Ann limping her way back home."

"We did not collect books but had many that were handed down. We have a collection of penny magazines from 1835. It came out every Saturday and was like an encyclopaedia. There's a very interesting section about decoys in one issue. It shows men with guns, which was inaccurate as guns were not used at all. It cost a penny and was published by the Society for the Diffusion of Knowledge". This Edinburgh-published magazine was very grandiose in its aims to educate a working class audience. It ultimately failed to keep its readership before failing in 1845.

Billy's interest in weaponry was not confined to guns. He also had a sword belonging to Cetewayo, the last great Zulu king, dating from the short Anglo Zulu war of 1879. He also had a sword stick and a silver-topped Regency dandy stick. Annie recalled that there was one on the cover of a Georgette Heyer novel that was almost identical to the one her husband had.

Annie liked historical novels – Jane Austen, Charles Dickens, Anthony Trollope – and although she had an old collected illustrated complete works, she did not really like Shakespeare. She remembered having to learn the 'Friends, Romans, Countrymen' speech from 'Julius Caesar' by heart when she was at school. She did like recitations and still has a collection of Tennyson's poetry which she received as a present when she was 21. Remember, too, she could still quote political slogans from the Boer War era and one of her favourites, Winston Churchill's "Fight them on the beaches" speech.

The last of the antiques she mentioned were the highly collectable metal fire insurance plaques she had. "I don't know how old they are, but they were there when I was born. If you had the wrong sign outside your house and there was a fire the company would not put the fire out. The two I liked best were the Phoenix one and that of Atlas." These fire insurance plaques can date back to the early 18th century and not having the correct sign could indeed lead to disaster.

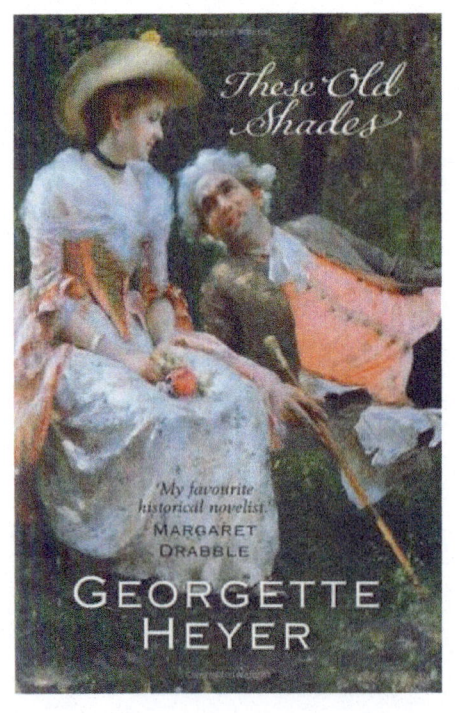

Annie's copy of the Georgette Heyer novel *These Old Shades*

Chapter 9

THE END OF A DYNASTY

◦⟨⟩⸻⟨⟩◦

Billy was the very last of the Williams Decoy men, the last male of the dynasty that had worked there for three hundred years. Cook and Pilcher give a wonderfully apt description of both Billy and Annie thus: *"He was intensely sociable and enjoyed the company of his fellow men; only Herbert and his wife can have equalled his and Annie's hospitality... he was ever willing to discuss the techniques of catching ducks and in the close season to show people around the decoy grounds of which he was immensely proud."*

"We always had three or four dogs. They were used by the decoy man to jump over the dog leaps and help with forcing the ducks along the pipes. Will's favourite was

Amber, a golden retriever. It only took a short time to train a dog for such work. The last dog we had, Bob, was a mongrel Alsatian mix. He was very intelligent and only took five minutes to train."

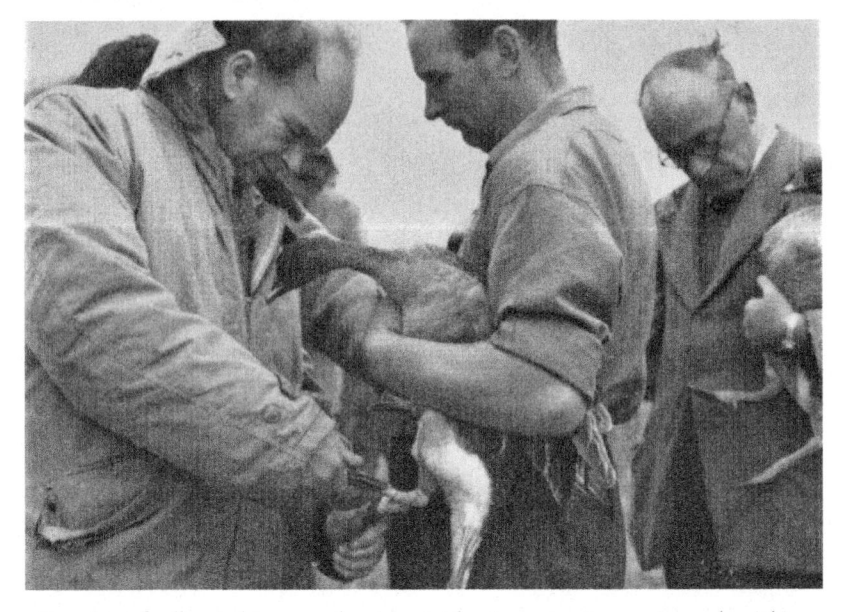

Peter Scott finally gets his way as he assists in the ringing, ageing, sexing and weighing of the birds.

Billy Williams asleep in the sun with his two dogs, Nella and Amber.

"Will worked very hard in his final years in the creation of the Trust. I helped, too. They let me cut a ditch from near the house to join the pond. It was a miniature Suez Canal. We also planted lots of shrubs. Will sadly died just as we got the Trust going."

Will Williams was buried in the churchyard at St. Pega's, close to the Decoy where he had enjoyed so many years. He was a very well-liked man, which was shown when people from all over the country came to the funeral to pay their respects.

Annie continued to serve cakes and tea to all the visitors to the gardens with her usual cheerful style and continued to sell the odd painting too.

The Williams with their dogs by one of the Decoy pipes

Annie saw out her days at Peakirk working for the Wildfowl Trust until her walking was severely restricted and the use of walking sticks introduced. There were annual open days that Tony Cook used to run which Annie took part in.

I sincerely regret not writing this sooner nor seeing her at least one more time to say a big 'Thank You' to a very special lady. She died on 30th December 1986 aged 96, having had a most interesting life at a time when the world was changed for ever. She joined her beloved Will in St Pega's Churchyard in Peakirk.

As I said, at the beginning, I do feel very privileged to have met her and finally to have shared her story.

Rest in Peace

Annie and Billy's gravestone at St Pega's, Peakirk

Postscript

I had occasion to contact Ann Fletcher (née Harris) who is the granddaughter of Mr Arthur Ernest Harris, the person who bought the Decoy Farm, house and the duck decoy by auction in 1940. He was a Newborough farmer all his life and the Decoy became one of his farms. The conditions of the sale permitted Annie and Billy Williams to continue renting the farmhouse and the Decoy, which they did until 1949. This seems to have been a generous and sympathetic gesture.

Sam and Mary Harris married in 1948 and did not move into their new home until the following year, leading to the departure of the Williams. Sam and Mary were the parents of Ann Fletcher and Jane Harris, who lived at the farmhouse until her parents' deaths in 1992 and 2007. Ann had moved out in 1976 and lived in Newborough in her grandparents' house.

The Decoy farm and other farms in the area are run by Ann's three sons with Simon, the middle son, living and working the Decoy farm. Ann's hope is that one or more of her grandchildren will take over in the future. Is this the beginnings of another long standing dynasty? It would be good to think so.

As mentioned earlier in the text, Tony Cook assumed the mantle of decoyman after Billy's death in January 1958. The Wildfowl Trust took over the lease of the Decoy, with Tony in charge. The ducks were caught and ringed for data, which was sent to the Wildfowl Trust at Slimbridge and the British Trust for Ornithology. After Tony's death, Ivan

Newton, who worked for the Wildfowl Trust, became the new decoyman.

With the discovery of this figure, who turned out to be the very last decoyman, I was forced into writing a new subtitle for this book. The original idea was "The Last of the Borough Fen Decoy Folk", referring to Annie in that role as the last of the Williams family. Ivan, as I belatedly found out, was in fact the real last of the decoy folk. Despite his brief tenure in the job, it gave me no option but to change the subtitle to "Last Of A Fenland Dynasty". This emphasises the fact that Annie was the last in the long line of the Williams family, which is the main subject of the book.

Ivan worked hard, though at a less pressured rate than when the Decoy was in its heyday, as bird numbers had declined. He continued in this role until his retirement in 2016.

There is no longer a decoyman. There is no more ringing being done. However, to their credit, the Harris family are continuing to maintain the Decoy themselves. The boathouse and one of the eight pipes are being maintained as they were. The remaining pipes are being slowly dismantled, but the pathways are mown and access kept clear.

The Harris family are continuing to maintain the site and have no intention of allowing it to become derelict, but naturally it is no longer open for visitors. It is certainly good that at least part of our national heritage is being preserved. The work of the Williams family is not totally forgotten.

Appendix A

BOROUGH FEN DECOY FARMHOUSE

BOROUGH FEN DECOY ROAD Decoy Farmhouse TF 10 NE 4/113 II 2. Late C18 brick house, roughcast rendered. Thatched roof with coped gable ends. Two storeys. Three window range. Modern casements except for first floor centre which is C19 two-light gothic casement. Two modern ground floor canted bays. Central doorway with rectangular fanlight with intersecting glazing bars, glazed door and iron trellis porch. End stacks. Gabled wing at rear with thatched roof forming L-shaped plan. VCH Northamptonshire Vol II mentions the celebrated Decoy Farm, owned for many years by a family named Williams. An old wildfowl decoy is situated about 350 yds to the south-east.

The Decoy farmhouse in 1990

Appendix B

CLOSURE

SALE – Former wildfowl haven has new owners – but who is it, and what will they do?

Mystery as buyer seals Peakirk deal

THE EVENING TELEGRAPH news & advertising 01733 555111, classified 555222, www.peterboroughnow.co.uk
Thursday, July 3, 2003

GARETH ROSE NEWS REPORTER

FOR generations, bird-lovers came to Peterborough to wonder at the variety of wildfowl at one of the city's top tourist attractions.

But now mystery surrounds the new owner of the 10-acre Peakirk waterfowl site.

The deal, which has been finalised after a year of negotiations, also includes 25 acres of surrounding wetland.

The site was closed in December 2001 by the East of England Agricultural Society, which had leased it from the Slimbridge Wetland and Wildfowl Trust for a decade, but could no longer support it.

Today, Robin Clarke, of city lawyers Smiths Gore, which handled the sale, confirmed it had been bought but refused to reveal the identity of the new owner.

He said: "They (the buyer) have been interested from the beginning.

"We've had a variety of inquiries from people with a number of different uses in mind."

When the site was closed, staff were spotted rounding up the birds and transporting them to the trust's nine other sites across the country, which funds the sale will support.

But residents have seen some of the varieties of wildfowl return to the gardens since then, and say bird-watchers still turn up at the gates to watch them.

Mr Clarke would not say how much the land had been bought for, but Reinhard Biehler, the owner of Baytree Nurseries, in Spalding, and a forerunner in the bidding process, had been prepared to pay £250,000 before pulling out of negotiations.

However, he said the buyer has promised to be "sympathetic" to its history as a nature reserve.

Today, one supporter of the wildfowl site, Janet Quinn (59), of St Benedicts Close, Glinton, said: "I'm glad someone's bought it.

"But what are they going to do with it? That's what I want to know.

"Are they going to open it as a centre again? Or will they keep it for their own private use? It's so important to Peakirk, because this end of the city really has nothing else."

gareth.rose@peterboroughnow.co.uk

SHUT: Above, a closed sign hangs on the gate of the Peakirk waterfowl site.

BIRD: One of the flamingoes that used to call Peakirk home.

The sad closure of the Wildfowl Trust at Peakirk December 2001
(*Peterborough Evening Telegraph* report)

The Wildfowl Trust had become The Waterfowl Gardens after being leased to the Peterborough Agricultural Society in 1991 for a six-year period. Visitor numbers had fallen and, in 1989/90, the decision had been made by the WFT to sell. This move by the Agricultural Society also proved to be economically unviable and the site was closed in 2001 and in 2003 it was bought by a private owner, in whose hands remains. No birds were harmed. Those that were still present were all rehomed.

Rather than end Annie's story on a sad note, I want to look to the future. I suspect that the whole Williams family, going back to 1670, might have been turning in their graves if they knew of the demise of the actual Decoy. The Harris family, however, have vowed to preserve part of the old Decoy, so all is not lost.

The local Parish Council has, in its wisdom, put into action the Peakirk Neighbourhood Plan 2016–2030 and I have permission to quote selected sections from this plan, much, if not all of which I know that Annie would certainly have approved of.

Appendix C

LOCAL AREA MAP

Map showing the main areas (apart from London) around which the story takes place. You will see, marked in red, the position of the Decoy and its proximity to Peakirk. The road system is the modern one and would not necessarily have been the same in 1890 when Annie Williams was born.

Appendix D

THE WILLIAMS FAMILY TREE

The names of those associated with decoys and the decoys with which they were associated are in capitals.

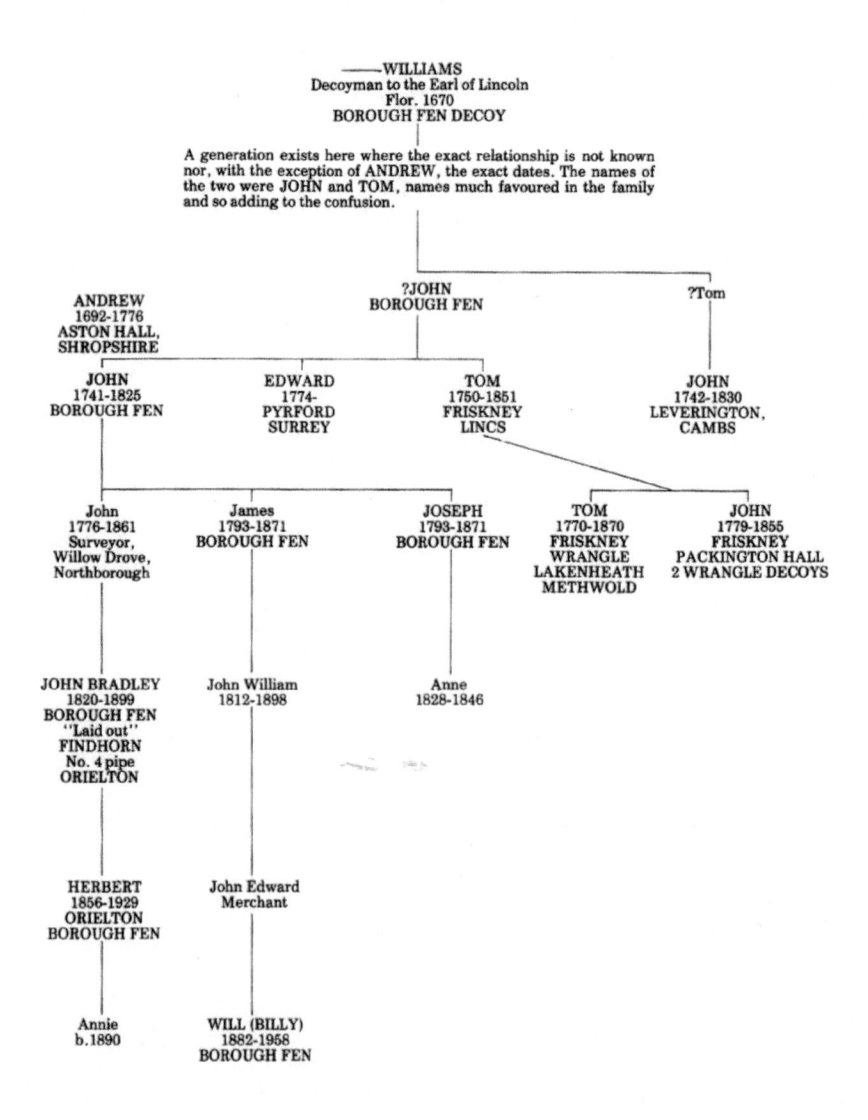

```
                        ——WILLIAMS
                  Decoyman to the Earl of Lincoln
                            Flor. 1670
                      BOROUGH FEN DECOY
```

A generation exists here where the exact relationship is not known nor, with the exception of ANDREW, the exact dates. The names of the two were JOHN and TOM, names much favoured in the family and so adding to the confusion.

```
    ANDREW              ?JOHN                              ?Tom
    1692-1776        BOROUGH FEN
    ASTON HALL,
    SHROPSHIRE
```

ANDREW	JOHN	EDWARD	TOM	JOHN
1692-1776	1741-1825	1774-	1750-1851	1742-1830
ASTON HALL, SHROPSHIRE	BOROUGH FEN	PYRFORD SURREY	FRISKNEY LINCS	LEVERINGTON, CAMBS

John	James	JOSEPH	TOM	JOHN
1776-1861	1793-1871	1793-1871	1770-1870	1779-1855
Surveyor, Willow Drove, Northborough	BOROUGH FEN	BOROUGH FEN	FRISKNEY WRANGLE LAKENHEATH METHWOLD	FRISKNEY PACKINGTON HALL 2 WRANGLE DECOYS

JOHN BRADLEY	John William	Anne
1820-1899	1812-1898	1828-1846
BOROUGH FEN "Laid out" FINDHORN No. 4 pipe ORIELTON		

HERBERT	John Edward
1856-1929	Merchant
ORIELTON BOROUGH FEN	

Annie	WILL (BILLY)
b.1890	1882-1958
	BOROUGH FEN

Reproduced from 'The History of Borough Fen' Tony Cook & R.E.M. Pilcher (1982)

Appendix E

THE PEAKIRK NEIGHBOUR-HOOD PLAN 2016-2030

"Peakirk was originally an agricultural settlement. Its sustainability was ensured by the best use of the agricultural land surrounding it. Originally this was Medieval fields to the north and west. The c1812 Parish enclosure map shows the position of large open fields called Dovecot Field, Well Moor Field and Tween Towns Field. Peakirk was part of the Glinton Manor and probably shared these fields with them. After the reclamation of the fenland to the east and south, large arable fields, diverted by drains, became the dominant landscape in this area. The coming of the railways in 1848, enabled fresh food, including ducks from the local Borough Fen Decoy and fresh goods brought by boat to be transported quickly to London."

This emphasises the role that the railway had in the success of the Decoy and its birds.

"The Ruddy Duck public house, built of stone, is one of the oldest surviving buildings in the village, with several similar style farmhouses that may be even older, such as The Goshams, also surviving." Mention here of Annie and Billy's last house reputed to be the oldest surviving house in the village..

One aim that Annie would definitely have given whole-hearted support to concerns the environment:

AIM 4: ENVIRONMENT To safeguard and where possible enhance the parish's rural setting and historic character. To support biodiversity and habitats of importance

OBJECTIVES

Preserve and enhance existing wildlife habitats. Protect existing homes from flooding. Safeguard trees, woodland and hedgerows important to the setting of the village. Encourage sustainable design. Preserve and enhance the historic environment.

The highly detailed plan has ambitions for the former Wildfowl Trust site, too:

To designate part of the Old Wildfowl Trust Site adjacent to the Conservation Area to protect and enhance the setting of the historic core of the village. This valuable habitat of wet woodlands, reedbeds and ponds is synonymous with the village of Peakirk and important to the early years of the history of Conservation. It is also identified as a Priority Habitat of Lowland Mixed Deciduous Woodland in the UKBAP 1994. This area should be preserved to allow its continued protection of local biodiversity, as identified in the Peterborough City Council Green Grid Strategy 2006.

Map 9b shows this very clearly:

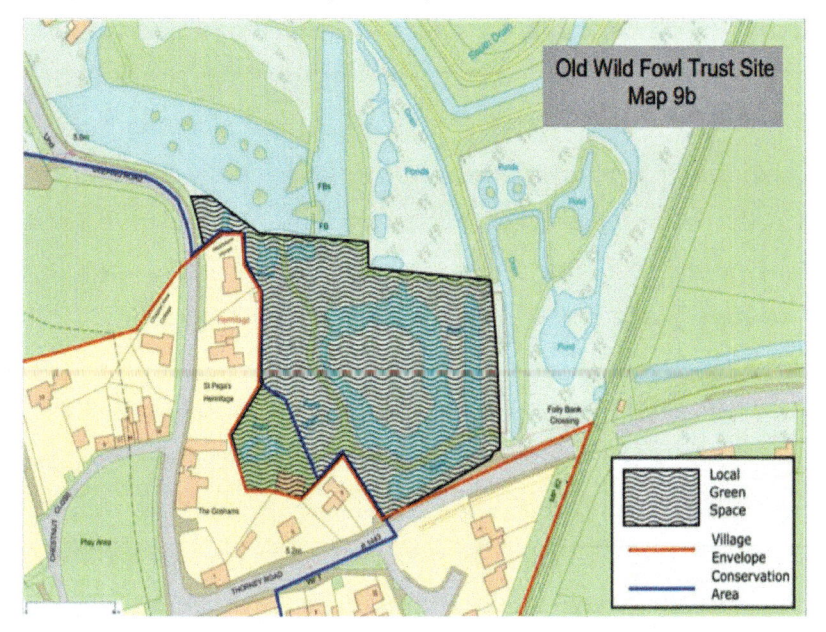

The importance of the former Wildfowl Gardens site must not be underestimated. After it formally opened in April 1957, there were 64,000 paying visitors per year by the mid-1970s, 8,000 of which were schoolchildren.

A detailed description of the 14 acres is described in a section headed 'Other Characteristics':

"The whole site was originally gravel workings, dug in 1840's for use on the Lincolnshire Loop railway line. 10 islands were constructed in the main pond. Once the gravel had been extracted, the area became extensive osier beds, used for basket making. In 1956 the site was purchased by the Wildfowl and Wetlands Trust and work started to transform it into one of their nine Wildfowl Gardens sites. The gardens were opened to the public, as the Trust's second centre, in April 1957 by Prince Henry, Duke of Gloucester.

Three more acres were added in 1967. There were 700 water birds, 108 species of which 5 were threatened with extinction. Our site has played its part in conservation history. It was the subject of a BBC East documentary in 1975 when Jean Goodman visited the scientific officer Tony Cook who explained that the numbers of Hawaiian geese had fallen to 28 in 1947, but Sir Peter Scott acquired a breeding pair for Peakirk, which went on to produce 1000 birds that were then re-introduced into the wild."

By the mid-70s there were 64,000 paying visitors, 8,000 of which were school children. Visitor numbers fell and in 1989/90 the decision was made by the WFT to sell the site. The Peterborough Agricultural Society leased the site in 1991 for 6 years, but it was uneconomical and closed in December 2001. It was sold into private ownership in 2003. The area as identified as needing special protection is the part of the site adjacent to the village Conservation Area. It contains the Ring Pond, which was the focus of Conservation work on ringing and cataloguing wildfowl, an area of wet woodland along the boundary with the B1443 Thorney Road which provides the setting for the Victorian cottages and a previous home to a colony of Flamingos and a belt of protected trees adjacent to the 10 islands pond which enhances the setting of the Hermitage Chapel.

There are, then, detailed long-term plans for Peakirk and the surrounding area. In keeping with the national and international move towards a green planet, this area could well be playing its part, albeit, in a small but not inconsiderable way.

Appendix F

MONEY CONVERSION

Understanding the monetary values mentioned in this book

Annie was born in 1890 and died fifteen years after UK currency underwent a dramatic decimalisation process on 15th February 1971. Most of her life, therefore, was spent dealing with pounds, shillings and pence.

A halfpenny (ha'ppeny) ½ d is worth 0.2083p

A penny 1d 0.4167p

Tuppence 2d 0.8334p

Threepence (thrupenny bit) 3d 1.25p

Sixpence 6d 2.50p

A Shilling 1/- 5p

A florin (two bob) 2/- 10p

Half a crown 2/6 12.5p

A Crown (five bob) 5/- 25p

Ten-shilling note (ten bob) 10/- 50p

The sum of 3/9d is mentioned in the text, which is the equivalent of 18.75p in today's money.

I will leave you to work out any others you encounter. Good luck.

Picture Acknowledgements

1. Will Williams Cottage photo by Paul Heath (erstwhile tenant)
2. Photo of Annie: Still from BBC TV interview with Jean Goodman
3. Diagram of 8 Pipe System 'Eye of the Wind': Peter Scott
4. Narrow Street Peterborough: Peterborough Images Archive
5. The Market and Cathedral, Peterborough: postcard
6. Peakirk Railway Station Peterborough: Images Archive
7. Adelaide Bassett: Peterborough Images Archive
8. Diamond Jubilee Celebrations: Queen Victoria postcard
9. Cliffs and Lighthouse: Hunstanton postcard
10. General Buller: button, Old Curiosity Shop (still available to buy for £15)
11. Advert for Laudanum: history.uk multiple sources
12. Advert Bile Beans
13. Peterborough Agricultural Show 1896, Ticket: Peterborough Images Archive
14. King Edward VII and Queen Consort Alexandra: *Daily Express*
15. Mr. W.H. Ewen: peterboroughtoday.co.uk *(Peterborough Telegraph)*
16. Ewen's plane: peterboroughtoday.co.uk *(Peterborough Telegraph)*
17. Crowd picture for Ewen: peterboroughtoday.co.uk *(Peterborough Telegraph)*
18. Coronation celebration for George V: Crowland postcard
19. Annie as Britannia: cropped from postcard
20. Harvest Floods, Crowland August 1912: postcard
21. Peakirk Roll of Honour: multiple sources
22. Francis Faithfull photo and war information: peakirkvillage.co.uk
23. Death in Belgium
24. The Monument, Peakirk: multiple sources

25 Light Armoured Motor Battery Car
    rgjmuseum.co.uk/photo-archive-item

26 Rook Pie recipe: *Mrs Beeton's Book of Household Management*

27 Haig at the Victory parade 1919: National Portrait Gallery

28 Motorized Charabanc of 1920s: Photo in the Book of Knowledge,1924. OCLC: 60401094

29 Hats in abundance: Peterborough Images Archive

30/31 Beau Geste/Gone With The Wind film posters: Pinterest multiple images

32 The Hippodrome, Peterborough: Peterborough Images Archive

33 Peterborough Pavilion Rink: Peterborough Images Archive

34 Coronation Celebrations, Peakirk: 1937 postcard

35/36 Young Viking Statue, Peakirk: Stills from BBC TV interview with Jean Goodman

37 Peter Scott with Annie: photo permission given by Ann Fletcher

38 Peter Scott photo 2: wwt.org.slimbridge

39 'Black Ducks at Noon' Scott painting: Approval to use given by Peter Scott

40 Annie at the Decoy Farmhouse: photo permission Ann Fletcher

41 Zena Dare, picture card Wikipedia, free to use

42 Sorry No Potatoes: multiple sources

43 Red Cow inn, Milking Nook, Newborough: newboroughvillagehall.co.uk

44 Decoy Farmhouse photo: permission Ann Fletcher

45 Billy Williams repairing a pipe at Borough Fen: Anne Cook, History of Borough Fen Decoy

46 Trinity Bridge, Crowland: multiple sources

47 Map showing the flood site, Crowland 1947: Phil Green, Peterborough

48 Photo showing flooded area, Crowland: heritagesouthholland.co.uk

49 Jackson and Williams, owners of the Decoy Farm House 1919-49

50 Retrieved plaque showing the opening of Wildfowl Trust, Peakirk: photo courtesy of Sally-Ann Jackson

51 The Goshams, Annie's Peakirk house: still from BBC TV interview with Jean Goodman

52 The Goshams back garden with the pond that Annie helped to construct. (photo courtesy of Colin Paterson)

53 Cover of Annie's Georgette Heyer novel *These Old Shades*

54 Peter Scott ringing, ageing, sexing and weighing the birds (photo courtesy of Colin Paterson)

55 Billy asleep with two dogs, Amber and Nella: Anne Cook, History of Borough Fen Decoy

56 The Williams with their dogs: photo permission Ann Fletcher

57 Annie and Billy's Gravestone at St Pega's, Peakirk: private photograph

58 Decoy Farmhouse 1990: photo permission Ann Fletcher

59 App A Decoy Farmhouse plan

60 App A Decoy Farmhouse photo

61 App A 2nd Farmhouse photo

62 Newspaper article on Wildfowl Trust closure: *Peterborough Evening Telegraph*

63 App C Local Area Map

64 Williams Family Tree

65 Old Wildfowl Trust Site Map 9B Peakirk Neighbourhood Plan 2016 -30

Bibliography

History of Borough Fen, Tony Cook and REM Pilcher, 1982 Providence Press

Eye of the Wind Peter Scott 1966, Hodder and Stoughton

The Wildfowl Trust 1958-59, Hugh Boyd and Peter Scott 1960, Bailey and Son Ltd

Household Management Mrs Beeton 1907, Samuel Beeton

Peakirk Village Tribune, Issue 122

Peakirk Neighbourhood Plan 2016-2030

Index

Abdication *1936 Mrs Simpson* 89

Asquith and WW1 *Rationing 54/5, German Butcher Frank (Peterborough) 55/6, Billy called up 54-57, 1919 Peace celebrations, Field Marshall Haig* 69-71

Bassett, Adelaide *Tragic death* 26/7

Bodger, Nellie and Annie, *cycling friends* 53

Boer War General Buller *Relief of Mafeking, Paul Kruger, General Buller* 32-34

Borough Fen estate *sold, Mrs Hanbury* 117/118

Boulogne *1922 74, Cologne and Bonn (Germany), Hyperinflation* 74/5

Canada 60/1

Cetewayo *Zulu King's sword 1879* 133

Chamberlain, Neville *Adolf Hitler, peace in our time* 101/2

Churchill, Winston *Fight on the Beaches 102, The Home Guard* 103/4,

Gas masks 103, First Aid tests 104, Dunkirk, Dig For Victory 104'5, Rationing 108, ITMA 111, Lord Haw Haw 111, *return to power 1951 126/7, Iron Curtain* 127

Cook, Tony *Assistant to Will, Waterfowl Trust head* 94, 130, 138

Crowland *1897 Diamond Jubilee 28, George V coronation celebrations Snowden's Field 46/7, Floods 1912/13 51/2, End of Great War celebrations 65/6, Rook shooting 67, Forester's Hall 79, Coronation 1937 89/90, Annie's view of Crowland 121/2, Trinity Bridge, The Ship*

Dame School *Lincoln Road East, Miss Pope* 22, 24/5, 32

Dare, Zena, *Roller skater actress* 100

Decoy, the, *Poultry business 42/3, First car 43, Wilfred Pickles Have a Go 112, Tennis and Bridge 115*

Doss House, *Piano lessons 121/2, 1947 Floods, Farmer Whitsed 122-126*

Edward VII Queen Consort Alexandra *Alexandra Rose Day, Edward's death 45/6*

Ewen, WH, *First plane in Peterborough, Walton, Marholm 48-50*

Flappers *fashion hats 76/7*

Gable, Clark *RAF Polebrook 107/8*

General Strike *effect on local area 86-88*

George V *coronation, Crowland celebration 46/7*

Glinton *Primary School 21, 25, 79*

Gravestones *St Pega's Peakirk 138*

Hill, Arthur *50 years assistant at the decoy 118-120*

Hunstanton *Holiday with mother 31/2*

Kettering High School *Maggie, subjects, tennis, stilts, parlour maid, dance instructor*

London Norman Cross, Leadenhall Market, *Charing Cross Hospital, nursing, Hay*

Market/Regent Street, Robot play, Pygmalion

Market Deeping *Boots 119/120*

Money conversions 151

Newborough *baker 14, Red Cow (Decoy pub) 12, 24, evacuees 104/5, 24 land mine (WW2) 107 Ted Browning 114/5,*

Newton, Ivan *Last physical decoy man 140*

Northborough *Plane crash 106*

Peakirk *River Welland, water pumps 13, railway station 22/3, Diamond Jubilee 1897 Rectory Gardens 28-30, Sunday school 30, Great War Roll of Honour, Francis Faithfull 57/8, St. Pegas Church 58, Jackson and Williams 128/9, Harris family Sam & Mary 139, (Ann Fletcher) 139, The Goshams 131, antiques collection 132-4, Excavation of garden for a pond 131, Waterfowl garden 129, 131, Neighbourhood plans 144, 147-50*

Peterborough *Cumbergate 11, Peter Brotherhoods 14, 107, Barrett's/ Shops 14, Cash station (Claribus) 15, Market 16, Dentist 37, Turner's Fish 'n' chips 16, Boongate 22, North Station, Trams 22, Bull Inn 24, Diamond Jubilee, Mayor John Thompson 29, Agricultural Show 43/4, Cinema 70, Palace Picture House 82, Hippodrome, Pavilion 82/3, Embassy Theatre 112, Penny Bazaar, Ice skating 84, Art School Mrs Kant 98*

Plough Monday 50/1

Queen Elizabeth II *Princess Margaret 127, Peter Scott commentary on Coronation 1953 127, Slimbridge 1963 127*

Queen Victoria *Diamond Jubilee 28, Funeral arrangements 35/6*

Ramsay MacDonald *Labour PM 75*

Rook Pie *Mrs Beeton recipe 68*

Scott, Peter *'Eye of the Wind' 1, Baxter shooting incident 68/9, Borough Fen Decoy 91, Kathleen and Edward Hilton 91/2, Trinity College Cambridge, Young Viking, Oundle School, 1936 Berlin Olympics, Life at the decoy 92, Punt gun 93, Royal Academy, Samuel Hoare 95, 97, Christmas at the decoy 101,*

Skegness *Holiday 32*

Tied Cottages *Decoy workers 12*

Votes For Women *Representation of the People Act 1918, Equal Franchise Act 1928, 78*

Wall Street Crash *1929, 88*

Wildfowl Trust *work of Peter Scott 129, 144*

Williams, Andrew *Epitaph 8*

Williams, Elizabeth Ann *Annie's mother, Household organisation 19/20*

Williams, Herbert *Annie's father's prowess as a decoy man 17/8, Crowland and Cowbit Washes 18/9, ice skating, Turkey Smart 19, Tram confrontations 23/4, Bull Hotel 79*

Williams, JB *Surveyor to Soke of Peterborough, Annie's grandfather, Typical Victorian beliefs*

Williams, Will/ Billy, *Canada foot incident 60/1, Mesopotamia, Army Service Corps, Basra, malaria, Seaforth Highlanders, Hero status 61-65, Wedding 1920, Honeymoon 71-73, Will's dogs, Bob, Nella and Amber 135-137*

Printed in Great Britain
by Amazon